365 Days of Affirmations

to

Restore your Joy

Compiled by

Dr. Vernessa Blackwell

&

A Host of Phenomenal Authors

Published
by LUI Media
P.O. Box 491
Waldorf, Md 20603

ISBN: 978-1-961743-10-6 Paperback
978-1-961743-09 0 EPUB
Printed in the United States of America

Edited by Katherine Anderson -Literary World Set in Eb Garamond
Cover Designed by Nadia Monsano

Library of Congress Information available upon request.
Published by LUI Media
P.O. Box 491
Waldorf, Md 20603

In the hustle and bustle of life, joy often finds itself buried beneath layers of responsibilities, worries, and routines. Yet, deep within each of us, there resides a wellspring of joy waiting to be restored.

This Journal invites you on this journey towards joy restoration, guiding you through reflections and practices that will illuminate the path to a more joyful existence from 365 Phenomenal Coauthors from across the globe.

As you embark on this journey, may you rediscover the joy that is inherently yours. May your heart be lifted, your spirit renewed, and your days filled with a radiant joy that emanates from within.

Table of Contents

Let's Start the Journey.....

Abdulrazak Abubakar

Abdulrazak Abdulrahman Abubakar is a Master of Financial Engineering candidate at the University of Johannesburg, holding a BCom honors in economics and a certificate in artificial intelligence and blockchain. As the President of the National Association of Nigerian Students in diaspora and South Africa. Connect with him on Facebook (Razi Abubakar), LinkedIn (Abdulrazak Abubakar), and Instagram (Razi_Abubakar).

AFFIRMATION

I am a resilient soul, transforming pain into strength, and mistakes into milestones. I embrace forgiveness, release the grip of the past, and unveil my identity. In purpose, I walk with intentionality, guided by the breakthrough that reshapes my life. I am a testament to redemption.

Felicia Alexander-Branch

Felicia Alexander-Branch is a native of Port Arthur, TX. She is a self-published author and the owner of Black Angel Publishing & Media. She is passionate about helping people understand self-publishing and operating a publishing company. Writing is my favorite pastime, passion, and strength.
Contact information https://linktr.ee/dependableangelservices and https://instagram.com/blackangelpublishingzandmedia/

AFFIRMATIONS

I am confident.
I love my life.
I am worthy of everything I desire.
I am manifesting the life that I desire.
I love myself.
I love my family.
I am grateful for my mindset.
I am proud of where I am and proud of where I am going.

Esther Adebayo

Esther Adebayo is a child of God, a youth's advocate, a Preacher's Kid, and a Soldier in the U.S. Military.

She has served in the Writer's club and has a deep longing for the Women's Ministry. Please connect with Esther on YouTube at https://www.youtube.com/@missus_gold or via email at adebayonike24@gmail.com

AFFIRMATION

I believe in the qualifying power of the Lord over my life. Henceforth, I walk away from the place of doubt, into a position of divine clarity. I receive the grace to be fortified and deeply rooted in the report of the Lord for my life. Amen

Lakisha Adams

Lakisha Adams, Retired Air Force, a tenacious, dynamic, visionary with a stellar 25+ year Human Resource Management record of success in leadership, change-management, and creative problem-solving to operationalize strategies uniting diverse mission sets. She enjoys public speaking and serving the community while inspiring others to be uplifting and positive influences.

AFFIRMATION

U (Uplift), P (Positive, say something positive about yourself),
L (Love, show yourself some love as God has blessed you with this life),
I (Inspire your two cousins; you're battling breast cancer together),
F (Fight this battle with God. You're not alone; he strengthens you),
I Thank God for today.

Evangelist Nicole Adkinson

Evangelist Nicole Atkinson is a two-time Author and Evangelist Nicole Adkinson is a businesswoman who walks in divine authority in the Marketplace. She is the founder of *Women of Courage Ministries*, an intercessory prayer ministry.
Nicole is also a Multi-Unit Manager for a National Optical Retailer and an Inspirational Leadership Speaker and Coach.

AFFIRMATION

I am joy. Joy is my portion. In Your presence Lord there is fullness of joy. I find joy in uncertainty. I deserve to be happy. I accept joy. Joy is a part of my life. Joy leads me to all happiness. Joy is my portion. Joy is my friend.

Dr. Anthea Aikins

Dr. Anthea Aikins is an ordained Elder, a certified Spirit-led Christian Coach *(HIScoach)*, a published Author, a Microbiologist, an Associate Professor, and a S.T.E.M. Academic coach. To find out more about her services, visit her at www.aaikins.com | Company: AAIKINS LLC

Website: www.aaikins.com | Email: Excellence@aaikins.com

AFFIRMATION

I AM Who God Says I Am!
I AM Not Alone! God Is with Me- *Deuteronomy 31:6*
I AM Preserved by God from All Evil - *Psalm 121: 7*
I AM Deeply Loved by God. – *Romans 8:38-39*

Israel Akinloye

Israel is a trained educator who is passionate about youth development and a graduate of the University of Lagos, Nigeria. He has experience in training youths in digital and freelance skills, and he offers brand and website design services as a CEO at Peptchris Media. He is an active volunteer in several community-focused organizations and a co-founder of a youth-led NGO focused on teenage mental wellbeing.
He can be reached on all social media handles @abukunolu and digitallyisrael@gmail.com.

AFFIRMATION

Although my thoughts may not always be the thoughts of the Lord, and His ways may not be as mine, I affirm that I rejoice in His words and that He is making all things work for my good.

Rev. Dr. Patricia Allen

Rev. Dr. Pat Allen | FB. Patricia Rester Allen Revpaallen@aol.com | 254-892-9052 Dr. Allen is a board-certified licensed Christian counselor. She resides in Dallas, TX. Her mother was a 14-year-old victim of rape. Dr. Pat is a widow and mother. She has devoted her life to helping survivors of rape. Her career culminated by teaching Bible Study at the White House and founding Prayer Shield Ministries. Rev. Dr. Pat Allen received Jesus as a savior at twelve. Her priorities are her relationships with the Lord and her family. She lives to see people changed and transformed by the presence of God. She was born to bring truth and a divine alignment of God's love to others.

AFFIRMATION

Be changed and transformed by the presence of God to bring truth and divine alignment of God's love to others.

Tangela Allen

Dr. Tangela Allen is a highly accomplished Alignment Coach, Author, Speaker, and the visionary behind Rhythms of Life Coaching. Her impressive academic credentials include dual Doctorate degrees in Educational Leadership and Organizational Leadership from Nova Southeastern University, and an honorary Doctorate in Philosophy from Trinity International University of Ambassadors.
FB: Rhythms of Life Coaching |IG: @rhythmsoflifecoaching_

AFFIRMATION

"In life's tapestry, woven with love and joy, I embrace moments of overflowing happiness. Despite heartbreak and unreciprocated love, I reclaim joy as an act of self-love. Amidst the pain, I choose to remember the shared joy and consciously fill my heart. I am resilient; I reclaim joy, one thread at a time."

____

____

____

____

____

____

____

____

____

Donald C. Alston Jr.

My Name is Donald C Alston Jr.
I was Born and reside in Flint MI
I Am a Man of GOD
I Am the Author of I Am Healed Walking in Faith
I Am a Certified life coach as well.

AFFIRMATION

I forgive myself for my past mistakes.
I Am grateful for my life.
My energy is magnetic.
I Am Wealthy.
I Am Healthy and happy.
I'm protected and loved.
I Am grateful for all that I have.

Tiffany Alston

Tiffany Alston, Co-Founder of The Self-Care Company, born and resides in Flint, Michigan.
Certified life coach, beauty & self-care consultant.
Author of *The Journey of Faith and The Transformative Power of Self-Care*.

AFFIRMATION

I Am Healthy. I Am Wealthy. I Am Beautiful. I Am Grateful. I Am Bold. I Am Confident. I Am Smart. I Am Thankful. I Am Love. I Am Joy. I Am God's Masterpiece.

Debra Anderson

Debra Anderson: I am a thirteen-year-old resident of Tennessee. One of my main goals in life is to grow in my understanding of the gospel and devotion to God as well as write as a journalist. I took this opportunity to gain writing experience and share my personal growth through devotion.

AFFIRMATION

Today I will take a step closer to what God has for me. When I am walking in obedience to God, I am always on track and never behind. If I trust God, big things will happen in my life. Every day is preparation for the new blessings to come.

Dr. Ivy Anderson

Ivy Anderson. D. Min., Ed. D., RN. I am a daughter of the Mississippi Delta, specifically Greenville, Washington County. I am a promoter of living life in abundance, to the fullest, until it overflows with the manifestation of health and wealth in every area of life. Contact information:ivyloupg@gmail.com

AFFIRMATION

I am love, joy, peace, longsuffering, gentleness, goodness, faith, meekness, and temperance. I think on whatsoever things are true, whatsoever things are honest, whatsoever things are just, whatsoever things are pure, whatsoever things are lovely, and whatsoever things are of good report because I have the mind of Christ.

Kamisha Anderson

I am a proud mother of four and I currently serve as a mental health therapist, behavioral coach, and death doula. I embarked on this journey of co-authoring with my teenage daughter, Debra, to show her that all things are possible, and dreams are just one breath away.

AFFIRMATION

The life I imagined is alive and has already been declared beautiful. I can relax knowing that it will pass in its perfect timing.

Le'Keshia Atchison

Le'Keshia Atchison who goes by the pseudonym "I AM Creative Words" is a 15-year Navy Veteran, Spoken Word Artist, and Author of 4 books (all published in 2023 and available on Amazon.) She is also the co-host of the Healing Soul Wounds Podcast (listen on Spotify and Amazon Music).

AFFIRMATION

Father, in the matchless name of Jesus Christ, according to John 7:37, "If any man thirsts, let him come unto me, and drink." Father, I am here asking for a drink to quench my thirst for __________ (fill in the blank). According to Matthew 19:26, I know with You nothing is impossible, so Father, I thank you in advance on this day for answering my request and having Your living water flowing out of my belly (John 7:38). I seal this prayer with the Blood of Jesus Christ for I know according to Revelation 21:6, "It is done". In Jesus Christ name! Amen!

____

____

____

____

____

____

____

____

____

Kimberly Babers

Kimberly Babers is an educator, published author, and a retired United States Army Veteran. Kimberly is an Ordained Evangelist, who believes in the empowerment of all people through the Word of God, Kingdom living, and the power of prayer. Connect with her on Facebook, Kimberly Babers

AFFIRMATION

Forgive and release, allowing the healing power of forgiveness to bring joy to your heart.

Njabulo Banda

Dr. Njabulo Banda is a South African social scientist and public health specialist with a wealth of experience in the management and coordination of community development and research projects. Her research interests include public and mental health, wellbeing, and African health strategies. She has published on health information, indicators of health, mental health, and health systems strengthening.

AFFIRMATION

I may be the first to do many things in my family, but I have started a legacy of excellence, blessings, and wealth which is contagious and will continue for generations to come. Lack is no longer the portion of those who will come after me.

Tanisha Bankston

My name is Tanisha Bankston. I am native from Grenada Mississippi. I currently live in Oxford, Ms. I am a believer. I am a mother of three children. I am one of God's chosen ones. I am an author, co-author, certified life coach, blogger, CEO, and founder of I Believe You Inc. nonprofit organization, and I have a private support group on Facebook for domestic violence and sexual assault survivors. The group is for women only.

AFFIRMATION

Speak to yourself every morning and say today I choose to be happy, free, loved, and living. Say I can overcome situations and negativity. I choose to be me.

Bartee Bartee

Bartee co-authored his first books with his wife.
"In The Beginning, there was God, Me & You".
They are recipients of the *Literary Award* from the FRESH Book Festival, presented by the Mayor of Daytona Beach.
Search for *Angie BEE & Bartee on YouTube on* Wednesdays at 7 pm EST www.Facebook.com/AngieBEEandBarteeProductions
www.BarteeSings.com

AFFIRMATION

Common sense is what me and my wife talk about all the time. When I say: "Common Sense", she says: "Everybody doesn't have Common Sense!" I say to her, if God didn't give me anything else, He gave me enough common sense to say:
"Don't Be Stupid – Keep Running!"

Dr. Shirley Boykins Bryant

Dr. Shirley Boykins Bryant is an Author, Youth Behavioral Coach and Chief Operating Officer of Let's Talk About It" – Behavioral Coaching LLC. She possesses a Doctorate in Human and Organizational Psychology. She can be reached via:

LinkedIn: linkedin.com/in/shirley-bryant-ph-d-44a7b1126
Twitter: Shirley84928799
Facebook: https://www.facebook.com/shirley.bryant.14
Instagram: https://www.instagram.com/shirleybryant626/
Website: https://lets-talk-coaching.com

AFFIRMATION

Resilience is the power within me to face life's challenges with unwavering strength and determination. I will embrace every obstacle as an opportunity for growth and learning. I will bounce back while becoming stronger and wiser in the process, thus, becoming the person I was destined to be!

____

____

____

____

____

____

____

____

Rhonda Berryhill-Castaneda

Rhonda Berryhill-Castaneda is a married mother of three in Southern California.

She is a child development expert and educator, business owner, author-certified life coach, and Infinite Possibilities instructor. Rhonda is proud to be a part of all four of the Joy/Devotional series.

AFFIRMATION

Let us build the city of God. May our tears be turned into dancing! For the Lord, our light, and our love, has turned the night into day!

Aharon J. Beavers

I am Aharon J. Beavers, or “AJ,” I was born to unite, and connect my generation.

The Local Tourist Craves LLC was designed to unite cultures and people through the universal language of food.

Please join me as I add value and vibrant flavors to the world!

AFFIRMATION

My moments of grief will not last forever.
Things don’t happen to me.
They happen for me.
My grief is not my identity.
I am healthy and healed daily.
I am divinely guided and protected.
Things will get better and lighter.
I will experience peace.
My experience will help others.

____

Gil Beavers

Gil Beavers is a Retired Air Force MSG / IT Specialist of RICH RELATIONSHIP REFUGE. Gil Beavers retired from the Air Force after serving 23 years and now is a four-times published author relationships coach and a podcast & YouTube creator and influencer.

He is a government employee; Gil also holds a BA in Business IT Management from WGU.

AFFIRMATION

So let us continue to press on, Rich Bro, the journey may be challenging at times, but with a heart full of joy and gratitude, we can overcome any obstacle that comes our way. Let's choose to find the beauty in each day and cherish every moment we have with the people we love.

Renée M. Beavers

Author/ Lifestyle Strategist of RICH RELATIONSHIP REFUGE Renée Beavers is an entrepreneur, a seven-times published author, relationships coach, podcast & YouTube creator, and influencer. This former 28-year salon owner is also a Lifestyle Strategist with a Plant-Based Nutrition Certificate from Cornell.

AFFIRMATION

YOU ARE LOVED
My Rich Sisters, I urge you to hold on to hope and never lose sight of the light that shines within you. Even after the deepest grief, joy can still find a way into your heart. Remember that you are loved by God and that you are never alone. Also, YOU ARE MORE THAN ENOUGH!
Love Renee

____

____

____

____

____

____

____

____

____

____

Evangelist Angie BEE

Evangelist Angie BEE is an International Best-Selling Author, a media and audiobook producer, and a motivational speaker. In 2023 she celebrated 12 years of ministry and 10 years of marriage. Together, they bring Mental Health and Alopecia Awareness workshops and book signings with live tour engagements.
Visit www.DaQueenBee.com www.YouTube.com/AngieBEEpresents and www.Facebook.com/AngieBEEproductions

AFFIRMATIONS

I asked my eldest daughter "What is an affirmation?"
She said: I am Strong! I am Cute!
I am Capable! I am Blessed!
I asked my youngest daughter. She said:
I am THAT Bitch! Thanks to my daughters, Angelyn, and Jasmine. Their differences make me LOL!

Karla Beedles

Hey Friend! I'm Karla Beedles, founder of Rich Girls HQ, speaker, and coach. I inspire and support women living RICH on purpose, every day! I'm a lover of God, wife to Cedric Beedles, member of Zeta Phi Beta Sorority Inc., shopaholic, and friend to many. Let's connect on this journey to A Lifestyle Reimagined!
@richgirlshq (Instagram & TikTok)
www.facebook.com/groups/richgirlshq (Facebook)
www.richgirlshq.com

AFFIRMATION

I live each day intentionally, with purpose and determination. I embrace and celebrate my uniqueness, as I fearlessly pursue the life of my dreams. Today, I choose to live my life, my way. I am worthy of A Lifestyle Reimagined.

Khadisha Benjamin

Khadisha Benjamin is a U.S. Virgin Islands native residing in NJ and the mother of two beautiful children. She is a spiritualist and health practitioner who finds purpose in utilizing her life experiences and ingenuity to healthily impact humanity.

AFFIRMATION

I am that I am and that is enough.

Dr. Jo Anna Bella Bennerson

Dr. Jo Anna Bennerson holds a Ph.D. in Business Management/Leadership earned in 2021 from Capella University. Dr. Bennerson has over thirty years of experience working in the financial industry and consulting in the government. Additionally, she has been featured in several anthologies.
Author_joannabella@yahoo.com

AFFIRMATION

With hopes to inspire you, Jo Anna Bella shares her favorite self-ordained quote with you, "Every decision you make is an action you take, and every action you take is a decision you make!"

____

____

____

____

____

____

____

____

____

____

____

____

Keri Bentsen

Keri is a Wellness Life Coach dedicated to empowering women to value themselves and guide them in prioritizing physical, mental, and emotional wellness alongside building a thriving life, so they can find joy again.

Email: keri@WellnessTweaks.com
Web: www.Self-Care.WellnessTweaks.com
LinkedIn: https://www.linkedin.com/in/keri-byrne-wt/

AFFIRMATION

I embrace my unique self with unconditional love and unwavering belief. I am enough, deserving of joy and living my dream, and I confidently prioritize my well-being, connecting deeply with my heart.

Denise Bethea

Pastor Denise Bethea is a humbled woman of God who was raised in what they called uptown Washington, D.C. Pastor Bethea is a widow. She is a mother to her one and only, 26-year-old young adult son, and a loving GlamMa. Pastor Denise has kept her feet to the fire! She is currently the CEO of Women of Worth

AFFIRMATION

I am beautiful and amazingly loved by God.

Dr. Vernessa Blackwell

Dr. Vernessa Blackwell is the Visionary for *Joy 365*, a Multi multi-international best-selling Author/Speaker, Grief and Joy Restoration Coach, and 24-year Army Veteran.
She is the Founder and CEO of Life U Imagined Media known as Dr. Vee, the Best-Selling Book Strategist and can be found at @www.publishwithdrvee.com or Twitter, Facebook, Google Plus, Linked in, and Instagram.

AFFIRMATION

I am greatly helped by God to help others. While I wait for my miracle, I serve so I am a miracle to others. I derive joy therein.

Artiana Bols

Artiana Bols: I am an Army veteran, devoted wife, and mother who transitioned from the uniformed field to safeguarding my family. Committed to excellence, I bring the same dedication to life and family. With the military behind me, I can look at life from a new horizon.

AFFIRMATION

I am a beloved wife and mother, navigating life's demands with grace. In every challenge, I find strength. My heart overflows with gratitude and joy blossoms in the ordinary moments with faith. I embrace each day, knowing that God's love sustains and restores my Joy.

Elder Jean Bonds

Elder Jean Bonds was ordained & licensed in 2008. She's an Actress, Author, Dancer, Entrepreneur and serves in many national & international ministries. She's the Founder of "Woman to Woman International Ministries" & "Connecting for His Purpose". Elder Jean & her husband reside in Maryland and this past June celebrated 27 years of marriage.

AFFIRMATION

I was chosen by God! God chose to breathe his air into my nostrils to wake me up this morning! I'm on God's mind! God cares about me! God favors me! God loves me! I am special to God! God, you are strengthening me daily! I am Victorious because of Christ Jesus! I am Loved! I am Joyful!
My Joy is contagious! Having an attitude of gratitude creates an atmosphere of joy. You are worthy of living a Daily Life of JOY!!! Say these Affirmations in the morning and as often throughout the day as you need it!

____

____

____

____

____

____

____

Phyllis Brewer

Phyllis E. Brewer is the owner and CEO of Trivashion Boutique located in Pikesville, MD. She has a keen eye for fashion and carefully handpicks merchandise that is unique in every possible way to help women step outside of the box and radiate their inner joy.

Affirmation of Joy:

1. I stand in the joy I create from within.
2. I am radiant, beautiful, and thriving.
3. I am vigorous, energetic, and full of vitality.
4. I am filled with positive, loving energy.
5. My inner joy is infinite, limitless, and abundant.
6. Joy is the essence of my being.

Antionette Broadnax

Antionette was born in Durham NC. She graduated from High School in Burlington NC. In her free time, she likes to travel and spend time with family.

AFFIRMATION

I wear joy as a coat as I go on my journey because this joy will swell up from within me like rivers of living waters. Therefore, I have no room for sadness, depression, and bitterness here after.

Allensia Brown

Allensia Brown is a devoted minister and founder of Her Crown Her Story Ministry and the Ariel Judah Agency. Based in Texas, she inspires others to live a life of purpose through faith, creativity, and empowerment.

AFFIRMATION

"I am filled with God's love, joy, and strength as I embrace compassion and understanding in my daily life. Through my connection with the Lord, I share His love and joy with others, creating a world filled with empathy, happiness, and spiritual growth."

Che Brown

Che Brown is a globally renowned giant in the sales world. He has cracked the code of entrepreneurial success with a game-changing model that unlocks unlimited financial potential, power, and wealth. He is the host of The Happy Entrepreneur Show (www.HappyEntrepreneurShow.com) and Founder of Comeback Champion (www.ComebackChampionSummit.com).

AFFIRMATION

Solutions Are Always Within Reach: The pandemic forced us to find innovative solutions and discover the boundless reserves of human creativity. It reinforced the idea that no matter the obstacle, there's always a path to joy and success.

Nui Brown

Nui Brown is a published author poet, screenwriter, and playwright who also works in the medical field.
Connect with her on Facebook, on Instagram @thenuibrownshow and LinkedIn.

AFFIRMATION

I AM COURAGEOUS

Bray Bryant

Bray Bryant is a 10th-grade honor student who attends Riverdale Baptist School. He is a member of the Spirit Band and plays on the HS Soccer team. Additionally, he is a member of Top Teems of America, Prince George's County, Sigma Beta Club, Phi Beta Sigma Fraternity, Inc.

AFFIRMATION

I declare that all the days of my life; I will dwell in the shelter of the Most High, finding rest in the shadow of the Almighty. My trust is securely placed in God, my refuge and fortress. I am safe and protected in His presence.

Dr. Angela Basden-Williams

Dr. Angela Basden-Williams is a Financial Literacy Campaigner *Life Insurance Agent* and Author
Website: https://wsbcampaign.com/angelabasden-williams
https://www.facebook.com/groups/1073046736516902/
Email: authorangela.mystrikingly.com
Email: Angelaabwfg@gmail.com

AFFIRMATION

I can do all things through Christ who strengthens me,
I am Blessed and Highly Favored,
I am confident, full of creative ideas and successful business owner,
I am a magnet for money and abundance,
I reflect trust and honesty in bringing knowledge, strategies, and solutions into the lives of others.

Juanita Banks-Whittington

Juanita Banks-Whittington, is a veteran, social worker, civil rights advocate, wife, mother, and author. She is excited to share her message through two inspirational books set to hit the shelves later this year. Connect and follow Juanita's journey as a new author on Facebook and Instagram, Nehi Cares LLC.

AFFIRMATION

My past does not define who I am today.
My boundaries and self-awareness will protect me.
I am worthy of my blessings.

Sherline Burnett

Sherline Burnett is an Entrepreneur, Speaker, Certified Christian Life Coach, Minister-in-Training, Educator, and Special Needs Parent Advocate. She is a mom of 4 and grandma of two grand-beauties. Sherline's favorite quote is "You were created on purpose, for purpose. Your Life Matters!"

AFFIRMATION

You were created on purpose, for purpose! Your Life Matters!

Dr. Lori Butler

Dr. Lori Butler is a mother of two beautiful children. Lori is a Texas native. She is a Best Selling Author, former Educator, and Business Owner. Lori is active in the disability and elderly community. Lori received a bachelor's, two master's degrees, in health, and business leadership. Lori's Doctorate degree is in business.

AFFIRMATION

Bloom wherever you are planted! This is one of my favorite affirmations, words found in Corinthians 7:21-24. Each one of us should take advantage of every opportunity for growth. Make the best of each day and live in the moment. Most importantly, always be grateful and humble.

Darlene Caffey

My name is Darlene Caffey, and I am the 8th child to the late Elder and Sister Sanders Edwards, Jr.
I am also married to Ernest Caffey, Jr., and we have 3 children. Additionally, I am a schoolteacher and a five-times published author. @caffeydarlene

AFFIRMATION

Today, I take authority over the giants in my life. Today, I will face them head on! Today, I will GO in the name of Jesus, knowing that the Lord will be with me!

Brianna Calhoun

Ms. Brianna Calhoun took the oath of office on 28 March 2022 as a Logistics Management Specialist. Born in Mobile AL, Brianna acknowledges Thomasville, AL as her hometown. In May 2021, she received her Bachelor of Science degree in Kinesiology. She is currently seeking her master's in business administration from Alabama A&M University. In her spare time, Brianna enjoys serving in her local church, spending time with her family, traveling, background singing, and participating in physical fitness exercises. Follow Me on Instagram @_foreverbriee and Facebook at Brianna Calhoun

AFFIRMATION

If I can quote one of my favorite gospel artists, Jonathan McReynolds, "…may your battles end the way they should, and may your whole life prove that God is good…" An Address to you (The Reader): May praise forever be your portion, for that is my secret weapon in all my life's struggles.

Dr. Shela M. Cameron

Dr. Shela M. Cameron is a visionary leader who is committed to her community. Through her leadership, survivorship, memberships, and entrepreneurship, she has accomplished many achievements. She shares her knowledge, volunteer time, mentors, educates, builds relationships with businesses, and provides resources and networks to promote opportunities for all. Dr-ShelaMCameron.com

AFFIRMATION

ALL MY BEST! The greatest accomplishments achieved while doing my BEST are as a single mother raising two respectful, college-educated, and trouble-free sons, retired military LTC of 34 years, best seller author - four books, recipient of BA, MS, PhD, presidential lifetime achievement award, entrepreneur, and many other awards and accolades.

Choose Joy

Robert Campbell

I'm a father, an author, and a veteran, I completed thirty years in the US Army. Along the way, I decided to write down my thoughts on the book of Revelation that I published in 2023, Apocalypse then and now, the Book of Revelation Revealed.

AFFIRMATION

May the blessings of the Lord Jesus Christ be upon you all and as you go through life's journey make sure before you offer words of encouragement to ask God before proceeding. Too many times we speak with the knowledge that our words may do more harm than good, but we offer our advice anyway without the consent of the Lord. So, before you respond, take a pause and speak to the cause through the lord Jesus Christ, and rest assured the advice given will be received in the spirit it was given.

LaRae Cantley

As an orator delivering messages to inspire collective action toward justice, I speak of courage, healing, and higher consciousness with a unique artistic flair. Bringing people from all walks of life together, practicing liberatory collaborations, creative artistic expression, and caring aloud is the heart of my offerings that fuel our souls to continue in this good work together. Creative Artistic Expression Video Podcast. Social media accounts; Instagram:l.a_rae Twitter: larae LinkedIn: LaRae Cantley

AFFIRMATION

Read (Psalm 82:3) & (Isaiah 1:17) It is our collective responsibility to uphold the joy in Justice for All. Fredrick Douglas Solidarity Statement. We are one with you under the band of prejudice and prescription, one with you under the slander of inferiority, and one with you in social and political disenfranchisement. What you suffer, we suffer. What you endure, we endure. We are indispensable and united and must fall or flourish together.

____

____

____

____

____

____

____

RaKail Carter

RaKail Carter is a native and resident of Little Rock, Arkansas. She is a wife, mother, and CEO of Kea to Beauty. She is a natural hairstylist who specializes in braiding and locs. She loves to help bring out the beauty in a woman and help them explore their inner selves. She's a huge believer and advocate for self-love. RaKail Carter is the KEA to beauty.

AFFIRMATION

SMILE! Smile as they speak on your name. Smile as they work overtime to tarnish your reputation. Smile as they pray for your downfall. Smile when God lifts you up. Smile when he speaks life over your aspirations and success. Smile through each battle. Remember, without a test, there's no testimony.

Dr. Melodie T. Carr

"Come. Make a statement. Leave. Be remembered." -Dr. Melodie T. Carr-
I am a mighty, praying Woman of God who through Jesus Christ has been forgiven, made new, and restored in God's abundance. I am a Veteran, SiStar, Sigma Phi Psi, Soror S.T.O.R.M., Oooahyeee! Connect with her @ MTCAgency@outlook.com.

AFFIRMATION

I will always be full of joy in the Lord. I will rejoice! I say it again, I will rejoice in it. The Lord is my shepherd; I have everything I need. Pour out your heart before Him; God is a refuge for us.

Darlene Caviness

Elder Darlene M. Caviness is a prophetic intercessor, conference and event speaker, and leader. She is the founder of the "Lord, Cover Our Seed" prayer community and launched the "I Survived It!" Conference in 2022. She is a certified Inner Healing and Deliverance Coach. She is the founder and CEO of Agilience Resources Contact AgilienceResources.com DarleneCaviness@gmail.com, info@agilienceresources.com

AFFIRMATION

The joy of the Lord allows me to walk in total victory.
I have the strength of God that enables me to overcome life's challenges and accomplish all my goals set before me.
I can do all things through Christ who strengthens me.

Dawn Charleston-Green

Dawn Charleston-Green is an award-winning author, wife, mother, and Veteran Army Officer, as well as a teacher, minister, blogger, writing coach, and speaker. Dawn uses her experiences and her faith to also provide valuable content and conversations for women, children, and families. Dawn is also the founder and CEO of Dawn of New Day 365, LLC. To find more of Dawn's writings go to www.dawnofanewday365.com. follow at Dawn of a New Day 365 on all social media platforms.

AFFIRMATION

I don't have to be what God has promised to be for me. He is my strength, my joy, and my peace.

Khalil Chase

Khalil Chase is a Business Major from Washington, DC. Currently in his Junior Year of college. His hobbies include trying new things. He takes pleasure in serving his community with community service. He is thrilled about this writing Journey.
Follow his progress on FB @Kaycwrites

AFFIRMATION

I start with a positive mindset.
I'm a King
I love accomplishing my goals.

Eunise Chery, CCLC

Eunise Chery is a certified Christian Life Coach, teacher, speaker, and author. Eunise is a Spiritual Mid-Wife Coach, who specializes in marriage restoration. Her passion is to help Christian wives birth joy during a broken marriage.

AFFIRMATION

I decide daily to choose joy no matter the circumstances.

Tisha Chin

My name is Patricia Chin. I am 57 years old, born in Kingston Jamaica to William and Iris Holness (Blessed memories). I have one sister and three brothers. One brother is a blessed memory. I attended Chetolah Park Primary School and Camperdown High School. I attended church at The Salvation Army where I was an active timbrellist and I was also a Brownie.

AFFIRMATION

I AM Grateful for every day of my life.
I AM beautiful and strong.
I CAN win, I must win, and I deserve to win.
I attract people to myself like bees to honey.
Peace is my Motto.
I AM who God says I am.

Dr. Michele D. Clark LMSW

Dr. Michele D. Clark, LMSW, CEO/Founder of LIFT After Breast Cancer LLC, draws from 20+ years of experience, degrees in Psychology, Social Work, and Honorary PhD, and her own story of resilience and triumph over Breast Cancer to empower high-performing female breast cancer survivors to Live Inspired Free & Transformed! Connect at info@micheledclark.com and www.linkedin.com/in/micheledclarklift/ to follow Dr. Michele

AFFIRMATION

During life's trials and tribulations, I have faith in God's promises which provide me with the strength to persevere.

Elle Clarke

Elle Clarke is the C.E.O. of ECM Global. She is a Bestselling Author, a Motivational Speaker, and the Founder of I AM QUEEN Magazine. Elle is married to Deangelo Clarke. They have four beautiful daughters: Jaylynn, Danielle, Eden, and Heiress.

AFFIRMATION

Dream Inspire Grow

Jasmine Christine Clarke

My name is Jasmine Christina Clarke. I'm going to the 7th grade and I'm currently 12 years old. I live in Belton, Texas, and I am the youngest girl of 3 older siblings. I have a younger brother. My favorite hobbies outside of school are dancing, cooking, reading, and writing.

AFFIRMATION

You are never too young to worship Christ.
Trust God All the Time.
Continue to pray for all things.
I am thankful every day for my life, my family, and my friends.
When I grow up, I want to be a teacher and a preacher.

Antron Cobb

My name is Antron Cobb and I was born in Winston-Salem, North Carolina. I am currently a Sous Chef for the Sheraton in Georgetown Texas. I have a beautiful wife and 4 beautiful children: Aniyah, Isaiah, Adrianah, and Harmoney.

AFFIRMATION

Thank you, Jesus, for the change in my life. Thank you, Jesus, for my family. Thank you, God, for everything.

Carolyn Coleman

I am Carolyn Coleman, a self-published author of non-fiction and a co-author of a #1 Bestseller anthology *Breaking Point when life requires a Shift*. My fiction turned into a series. I coined The Gentry Series. I once again have joined an esteemed group of authors in *She Said Yes to Herself Unapologetically*. I enjoy sharing my knowledge. I believe we can all win. The best time to start your goals is now. My website: CPWbookshelf.com

AFFIRMATION

Joy 365 Prayer
Heavenly Father, I thank you for the joy you have given me. This joy allows me to better represent you and brings others to seek you more. I thank you for allowing me to be a chosen vessel for Your Good work. … the Joy of the Lord is my strength. Nehemiah 8:10(NIV)

____

____

____

____

____

____

____

____

____

____

Chanelle Coleman

Chanelle Coleman is a bestselling author, playwright, speaker, visionary, and CEO of CeCi's Ink. As a survivor of abuse Coleman creates platforms that allow businesses and individuals to pour passionately and purposefully into women. Her movement motivates, inspires, and empowers women to walk within their God-appointed purpose. Find out more: @ www.shesaidyestoherself.com

AFFIRMATION

No weapon formed against me, whether it is a tool of the enemy, invention of man, or self-sabotage will prosper. I forgive myself for the things I did to cope while surviving traumatic experiences. I recognize my mistakes, but my shortcomings don't define me.

Whitney Coleman LICSW, LCSW-C

Whitney Coleman, LICSW, LCSW-C is a clinical social worker, therapist, author, and international speaker. Whitney is the founder and CEO of Jade Clinical Services. Whitney serves women of color to address life transitions and anxiety by helping them overcome barriers caused by intruding thoughts, stress, and trauma.

Social Media Information
Facebook: Whitney Coleman
LinkedIn: Whitney Coleman, LICSW, LCSW-C
Instagram: @jadeclinical, @whitneycolemanlicsw
Website: www.jadeclinical.com

AFFIRMATION

Today I embrace the gift of the present moment, recognizing joy is a choice I can make. I celebrate the small blessings that fill my day, understanding they are steppingstones to lasting happiness. I commit to actively inviting joy into my life, nurturing my spirit and well-being.

____

____

____

____

____

____

____

____

Dawn V. Collins

Dawn V. Collins is a native of California where she met her husband Terryl L. Collins. Together they have three brilliant, beautiful adult daughters. Dawn is the Founder and Doula of Birth Matters b/c Family Matters LLC. Witnessing clients realize their power is why Dawn is devoted to perinatal education. Connect with her on Facebook, IG, Twitter, and www.birthmttersbecause.com

AFFIRMATION

I allow the Holy Spirit to work and invoke love, joy, peace, patience, kindness, goodness, faithfulness, gentleness, and self-control in me as I choose to fix my thoughts on what is true, honorable, right, pure, lovely, and admirable. I think about things that are excellent and worthy of praise. In Jesus's name.

Sadie Collins

Sadie Collins is a Child Development Services Administrator with Child & Youth Services, with over 15 years of experience with children and ensuring that they have a safe and developmentally appropriate environment to grow and advance in. One of life's greatest joys is to see the expression on a child's face light up when they finally realize understanding and knowing. Ms. Collins was a member of the first team that obtained (NAEYC) Accreditation for a stand-alone hourly care program in the United States Army.

AFFIRMATION

I am a child of God, a daughter of the most-high King!

Dr. James JC Cooley

Retired Navy Officer, motivational speaker, author, and a television/radio talk show host of It's Your Life with Dr. James Cooley. Ph.D. and recipient of the 44th Presidential Legacy and 46th Presidential Lifetime Achievement Award. Born in Chattanooga, Tennessee, residing in Fort Worth, Texas, and Temecula, California, he is a husband, father, and grandfather.

AFFIRMATION

2My brethren, count it all joy when ye fall into divers temptations;
3Knowing this, that the trying of your faith worketh patience. 4But let
patience have her perfect work, that ye may be perfect and entire,
wanting nothing. (James 1:2-4 KJV)

Dr. Michelle Cooley

A financial services specialist, entrepreneur, and author whose specialty is in Marketing Management as Executive Producer and Co-Host of the television/radio show It's Your Life with Dr. James Cooley. A native of New York City, New York, she currently resides in Texas and California with her husband, Dr. James Cooley.

AFFIRMATION

"Martha, Martha," the Lord answered, "you are worried and upset about many things, but few things are needed—or indeed only one. Mary has chosen what is better, and it will not be taken away from her." (Luke 10: 41-42 NIV)

Teresa M. Cooper

Teresa M. Cooper is a nonprofit administrator, published author of three books, Pastor, and Creator/ Host of SisterFriends Cups and Conversations Talk show. Connect with her on Facebook, IG, womanofstature@gmail.com, and www.newcreationfamilychurch.com

AFFIRMATION

I believe my life is valuable and I am worthy of the pursuit of Joy. A Joy that is sustainable because I curate an authentic relationship with my Heavenly Father. I am full of Joy, I see Joy, I hear Joy, and Joy is tangible in my life.

Lakisha Copeland

Lakisha Copeland was born in Durham, NC., and graduated from the Illustrious North Carolina Central University in 2012 with a B.A. in Recreation Administration. In her free time, she likes to enjoy the outdoors, travel, hit the gym, and spend time with her lovely family.

AFFIRMATION

"Each day remember to go above and beyond for YOU."

Dr. Nina R. Copeland

Dr. Nina Copeland is a native of Montgomery, Alabama. She is currently serving in the United States Army. She is a certified Business and Entrepreneurship Coach. Dr. Copeland is a recipient of the Presidential Lifetime Achievement Award. She is married to Tarrance and a mother of three boys Terrell, Tyler, and Taylor. Connect with her on Facebook, DrNina Copeland, and at mwpcoaching23@gmail.com

AFFIRMATION

I am a conqueror! I will overcome the obstacles before me. I will accept and embrace my valley experience. It will not define me. I will identify God's purpose for my life. I will prevail.

Jen Chávez Perdomo

Jen Chávez Perdomo is a Personal Branding Strategist, professional Astrologer, Author, and Speaker. Connect with her on social media @rockastrobranding and www.rockastrobranding.com

AFFIRMATION

I deserve everything my imagination can dream of because I am ready and open to happiness. Now is the time to prosper and be great.

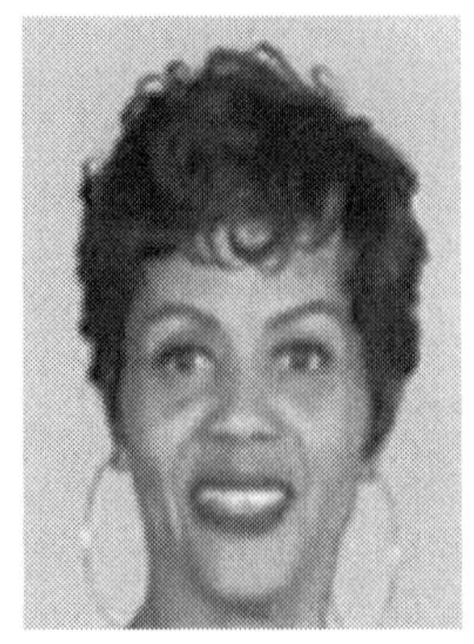

Sheila Conley-Patterson

Hi, I'm Sheila Conley-Patterson, I'm the CEO of S.C. Consulting Service LLC. We teach, train, and consult in wellness, behavioral management, GED, Youth Coaching, Notary Certified, and Motivational Speaking. We are dedicated to people from ALL walks of life. It is my PASSION. Email:
contractus@scconsultingservice.com
Business#:(414) 233-515

AFFIRMATION

Write the vision, make it plain Habakkuk 2:2.
We are treasure carriers that must invest in ourselves. Kneeology has taught us that the prayers of a righteous person can change a lot. Succeeding in what you were never asked to do will lead you to your gift and help you to find your why.

____

____

____

____

____

____

____

____

____

____

Sharon Coulberson

Sharon Culberson is, as always, smiling. Smiling is essential and laughter is medicine for the soul. She has a soft spot for at-risk populations, a diligent advocate for serving my community through volunteerism, caring for those in need, sharing knowledge, providing resources, and most importantly doing it all while attempting to make others smile.

AFFIRMATION

Blessed are those who mourn, for they will be comforted. Matthew 5:4 KJV

Death leaves a heartache no one can heal, but love leaves a memory no one can steal.

____

____

____

____

____

____

____

____

____

____

____

Jennifer Covello

Jennifer Covello is the founder of the Elevate the Day ministry. In her weekly podcast and blog, she shares how a close relationship with God will heal your heart and your life. Jennifer is an award-winning author, sought-after speaker, and mother of two young adults.

AFFIRMATION

I am God's Masterpiece, uniquely created for His purpose.

Deborah Crowley

Deborah Crowley is a successful business owner grossing over 1 million and a dedicated charity coordinator raising over $100,000. Her entrepreneurial drive and compassion have made a remarkable impact, inspiring others to give back. She is a true force for positive change, combining business success with philanthropy.

Exclusive Cleaning Services, LLC – https://exclusivecleaningservices.co
Exclusive Elderly Resource Center – P: 248-888-7806
Ladies of Justice – https://dcrowley39.ladiesofjustice.com

AFFIRMATION

I am a source of joy and happiness in my life. I embrace the beauty of every moment and find reasons to smile and be grateful. I attract positivity and radiate joy to those around me. I am deserving of happiness and allowing myself to experience it fully.

Dr. Darcele Marie Cole-Robinson

Darcele Robinson, is an educator, a published children author and has a nonprofit "Donation with Love Foundation". You can connect with her on nanadarcelestories.com and author_darcele on IG. Name on Facebook: Darcele Marie Cole-Robinson Instagram: author_darcele Website: nanadarcelestories.com

AFFIRMATION

TRY again. You can only fail if you stop trying. And lean on this truth- you CAN do this with the strength God gives you.

Takia Chase-Smith

Takia Chase-Smith is an Army Veteran, Published Author, and Publisher. She believes in encouraging and mentoring young women to achieve greatness! Her passion is healthy relationships. Takia can be found on social media under dreamkiaperspublishing. Her website is https://authortakia.mystrikingly.com. Connect with her immediately and share your thoughts about the read!

AFFIRMATION

I am a great parent! I will remain patient! I will remain firm and consistent! I will lead by example! I will ask for help from the LORD! I will express my feelings in descriptive words!

AJ Cuggy

Audrie is a novice writer. Her first book is in the works. She is a registered nurse, wife, mother, and grandmother. Audrie lives in the countryside of Montreal.
An avid reader, gardener, and animal lover are some of her passions. God, grandkids, pets, and family are her most important loves.

AFFIRMATION

Through grief and sorrow, joy and pain, God is always there. He holds me up. He gives me comfort, strength, and peace. Through Him all is possible. I pray to do his work each day. May my love of animals and mankind reverently serve the Lord our Father. Amen.

Siobhan Cunningham

Siobhan Cunningham is a US Air Force veteran, Licensed Clinical Social Worker, and devoted mother of two daughters. Her passion for helping others and her love for her family drive her efforts as a social entrepreneur and author.
Connect with Siobhan at https://www.linkedin.com/in/siobhandeann/ or on Instagram at https://www.instagram.com/empowerwomenveterans/.

AFFIRMATION

Practice self-care, honoring your well-being as a pathway to genuine joy.

TaiSheena Cunningham

Taisheena K. Cunningham is a wife, mother, grandmother, a professional educator as well as an entrepreneur. Most recently, she has become a Breast Cancer survivor and advocate to help women navigate the uncertain times during diagnosis.
Www.pamperedchef.biz/tai

AFFIRMATION

My Joy comes from within me, not the circumstances that surround me. "I choose Joy."

Pastor Michelle Curtis

I am a CHOSEN DAUGHTER of The King.
I submit myself as a willing and obedient vessel to be used for HIS Glory.
Here I am Lord, send me!
My past is forgiven by HIM,
My present is in HIM.
My future is secure with HIM.
IT IS ALL ABOUT HIM!

AFFIRMATION

I abide in the love of the Father and keep His commandments therefore my love is full. I rejoice in hope as I am patient in trials while being constant in prayer. I will remain in the presence of the Lord for in His presence is the fullness of joy.

Pastor Sheila Curtis

Sheila Curtis is a wife to a wonderful man of 21 years, and a mother to six adults, and one teenager. Sheila obtained her Bachelor' and Master's in Theological studies and became a certified Life Coach. Sheila loves the many gifts GOD has given her and plans to effectively use them all.

AFFIRMATION

Today, I operate knowing that my Faith, Joy, and Peace are Connected!

Marita Dabney

Mother, Grandmother, I embraced motherhood with Grace. Blessed mom of 8, I am a Super Mom and Grandmother. I pride myself on always creating a loving home and teaching my mini-ME's greatest Life lessons. One of my greatest accomplishments has been rearing my kids and getting them grown. In this I found Joy.

AFFIRMATION

God is bigger than whatever problems I have faced and am facing. God knows my name and every thought and has even numbered the hairs on my head. God cares about me more than He does the sparrows. I choose trust over worries. I choose trust over fear and so I choose joy as my new reality.

Dr. Doris H. Dancy

Dr. Doris H. Dancy, of Yorktown, VA, is an award-winning educator, speaker, writing consultant, editor, novelist, and musician. Her contact information is as follows: Website: www.dorishdancy.com Email: ddancy.pen2paper@yahoo.com Facebook: https://www.facebook.com/doris.dancy.9/

AFFIRMATION

It's important to remember that God's blessings are often actualized during a storm. We need not fear if we simply recognize His Perfect Plan, Understand His Divine Purpose, and Believe the Irrefutable Promises of the God of Abraham, Isaac, and Jacob.

Biodun Dapherede

Biodun Dapherede is the author of *Lead Me Past These Lies*, Pro Speaker, and founder of *The ImmiGreat Life*.
She is passionate about faith, family, and empowering individuals from minority communities.
Learn more at www.immigreat.life www.biodundapherede.com
IG: @immigreat.life||@biodundapherede
FB: Biodun Dapherede Author

AFFIRMATION

Joy and gratitude are permanent residents in my life and household.

Cynthia Davis

Cynthis Davis is a retiree with 25 plus years of government service with several agencies. She is currently a realtor and a recent graduate of Prince George's Community College Paralegal Certificate Program. She was a former co-author of #HLIC Head Ladies in Charge Book and Movie in collaboration with women across the world.

AFFIRMATION

Father, today I receive the Destiny Helpers that have been positioned in my life to help me fulfill the purpose and plans you have for my life. I receive your beauty for ashes and joy for mourning and your garment of praise for the Spirit of Heaviness as stated in Isaiah 61:3

Danita Davis

Danita Davis is a Licensed Mental Health Therapist and Founder of DaKal Wellness Solutions. She is passionate about removing the stigma associated with mental wellness, particularly in the African American community. She is relatable and transparent in her approach to empowering individuals and providing them with the tools necessary to overcome life's challenges.

Website: www.dakalsolutions.com
FB: facebook.com/dakalwellnesssolutions
IG: @dakalwellness

AFFIRMATION

"I am empowered through connections, navigating life's challenges with strength, resilience, and unwavering faith."

Susan L. Deal, Ed.S., INHC

Susan L. Deal is an educator, speaker, CEO of Radiant Living 365, Certified Holistic Lifestyle Coach, Meditation Teacher, and author of *Radiant Living: A Journey to Holistic Wellness* - a faith-based guide to self-care and personal development (available on Amazon). As a wife, mother, and grandmother (Sunny)to two special needs boys, she uniquely blends experience, education, and expertise to coach and support others on a path to radiant living – inside and out.
Connect with her on Facebook/LinkedIn: Susan Deal
Social media (IG/TikTok/YouTube/Pinterest): @coachsusan365

AFFIRMATION

"In the gentle dance of self-care, I nurture the divine light within, shining bright, creating a radiant path to my best self to share with the world."

Carla Ginebra De Garcia

Carla Ginebra De Garcia is the Founder/CEO of The Blue Line Angels Church (founded in October 2013). She is a Wife, Mother, Pastor, Professor, Chaplain with the Billy Graham Association Rapid Response Team, Author, and a Law Enforcement Officer with the Miami Dade Police Department since 2021. Her heart is mainly devoted to the restoration of the son/daughter's position of power and authority given by God since the beginning, protoevangelium—the first gospel.

Miami, Florida. | Cell 305-281-0760 Instagram @CarlaSaidYah, CarlaSaihYah.com @TheBlueLineAngelsChurch | thebluelineangels.com | linktr.ee/thebluelineangels | TheBlueLineAngels@gmail.com

AFFIRMATION

Miracles are happening in my life and through ALL generations! Today I prepare and be adorned with JOY each day because Greater is He that is in me, I see Heaven on earth, I see HIM coming again as my Bridegroom, Yeshua Hamashiach! The GREAT I AM lives in me!

____

____

____

____

____

____

____

Dr. Destiny

Dr Shante served in the U.S. Navy for 20 years and retired honorably in 2022. She is a combat veteran & wounded warrior. She received her PhD in Christian Administration and a Doctorate in Education and Leadership. She is an award-winning speaker, author, recovery facilitator, and transition consultant. www.drsdestiny.com https://www.facebook.com/DrShanteDestiny https://www.linkedin.com/feed/

AFFIRMATION

Doing It Afraid

1. I am not going to delay my destiny any further.
2. I will not wait for the absence of fear to pursue my dreams.
3. I am not going to get in my way.
4. For now on, I am doing it afraid.
5. I will fulfill my destiny every day.

Tyrone Dicks

Tyrone Dicks, 42, December 26, Born in Miami, Fl. Is a businessman that wears many hats. Poetry/Music are outlets, but Filmmaking is his passion. Film Projects will be attached below: Poem Books (Yang's Masculine's Nature {Release December 26} & Ying's Feminine Essence {Release February 14}, i.e. Www.BCMEINC.info

AFFIRMATION

I am Loved and Blessed.
All things work together for my good.

Tiphanie Thee Doll

I'm Tiphanie, a determined girl mom and aspiring entrepreneur on a transformative journey. Balancing the joys of motherhood with my unstoppable drive, fearlessly moving through the world of life and business, embracing every challenge as an opportunity. I am forging my path, inspiring others to chase their dreams while cherishing the beauty of motherhood.

Follow me:
Facebook: Tiphanie Nikeia
Instagram: TiphanietheeDoll
Website: theedollenterprise.com

AFFIRMATION

You Are the Prize, period! Your very uniqueness is what makes you the prize. Don't let anyone make you feel like because you're not doing it like everyone else, you're less than. However, you choose to do things YOU ARE THE PRIZE, period!

____

____

____

____

____

____

____

____

Milicent Driver

Milicent Driver is an empowerment strategist, author, and speaker. Her book, *Pretty Ugly: Strategies to Developing Your Mindset*, will encourage readers to take a personal inventory of their life ultimately leading to total self-love and acceptance. You may follow her. Facebook "Milicent the Strategist" and www.milicentthestrategist.com

AFFIRMATION

I'm choosing to trust in Jesus, even when life throws me curveballs. As a result of this act of faith, an unending river of joy is sustaining and encouraging me! By taking time out for God's presence each day, true contentment is available like never before - leading to long-term peace and satisfaction that can't be taken away.

Glendora Dvine

Glendora Dvine LPC BC-TMH has been a nationally accredited licensed counselor in Georgia since 2007 and in Michigan since 2021. Founder of Dvine Systems GA counseling agency in 2010. Glendora provides therapeutic counseling specializing in servicing individuals suffering from depression, anxiety, and trauma with expertise in EMDR and CBT modalities.

AFFIRMATION

We only have one life, LIVE, don't just exist. Expect the mess of life and keep it moving.

Denise E. Edwards

Denise is a mother of four and grandmother of two. She holds a Bachelor of Science and is certified as an Addiction and Crises Counselor. Most importantly she's a child of God with a calling as a mouthpiece for God to share her experiences, strength, and hope.

AFFIRMATION

Years ago, I decided to stop listening to and believing the
lies of the enemy and start declaring God's truth over myself. I declare I am "B.O.L.D".
B= Beautiful
O= Outgoing
L= Lovable
D= Deserving

Mrs. Benita M. Elcock

Mrs. Benita M. Elcock is a native of Washington, D.C. She has been a member of First Baptist Church of Highland Park in Landover, Maryland since 2010. Benita cherishes her role as wife and mother and she's deeply committed to helping others, she loves to serve. Her ministry is family counseling and guidance to young adults, Benita is also the author of the children's book "We Planted Seeds Today".

It is her mission to plant positive seeds in every interaction.

AFFIRMATION

I am A Child of God.
I am Safe.
I am Healed.
I am Happy.
I am Whole.
I am Peace.
I am Love.

Amber Enfinger

Amber Enfinger is an Accredited Event Designer, Wedding Planner and Designer, Realtor, and mom to three children. Connect with her on Facebook, Author: Amber Enfinger

AFFIRMATION

Cultivate a spirit of resilience, finding joy even amidst life's challenges.

Gloria Evans

Gloria is a retired Senior Underwriter with the State of California. She currently holds a license as a Real Estate Agent and a Consultant. Gloria finished her Ebook as an Amazon Best Seller in 2022. www.selftalkthepowerofrightwords.com, which is biblically based on how to talk better to yourself.

AFFIRMATION

Psalms 51:12
Restore unto me the joy of thy salvation and uphold me with thy free spirit. When we realize how much God loves us, and He will go to the ends of the earth to bring us back to Him, we can restore joy.

Pastor Kaye Ross Faison

Pastor Kaye Ross Faison is the Founder and CEO of Kaye Faison Ministries, known as KFM, located in Blythewood, SC., which serves as a beacon for hurting and mishandling women. Connect with her on Facebook: Kaye Ross Faison or at: www.kayefaisonministries.org.

AFFIRMATION

Today is a new day to succeed and to progress. I will move forward and become that which God says I am. I will not be discouraged or feel hopeless, when I have a God that is bigger than any situation. Therefore, I will Live and become better.

Dr. Blanche Farrish

Dr. Blanche Farrish is a minister in Pastoral Counseling (DMIN), Altar Counselor, Crisis Text Hotline Counselor, Community Chaplain, Mental Health Aid, Author (Amazon) God's Power
You can find me on fb@Blanche Farrish

AFFIRMATION

All my life God has been faithful, and all my life God has been so good. His goodness keeps running after me. Every breath I take I will sing of the goodness of God.

Artisa Felder

Artisa Felder is a mother, author, advocate, and business owner. You can contact her by email at artisamarie@gmail.com. Follow our author page to stay updated on new releases. Amazon.com: Artisa Marie: Books, Biography, Blog, Audiobooks, Kindle and follow us on Facebook @youareartisaandalonni to join the monthly journal challenge.

AFFIRMATION

God, I PRAISE you today for your amazing grace and mercy.
The JOY of the Lord is my strength (Nehemiah 8:10)

Author L. Fitz

Author L. Fitz is an esteemed author in four published anthologies, is a native of Little Rock, Arkansas; she resides in Irving, Texas with her husband. Fitzgerald is an astounding leader who loves to motivate women and share her knowledge to help them grow lead positive lives and put themselves first. www.authorlfitz.com

AFFIRMATION

I am strong and healed! I am no longer brokenhearted and crushed! I live for God because He is my everything! He is the only thing constant and permanent in my life! He gives me strength daily! My spirit is overjoyed and happy! I am LOVED!

Kemonte Fleet

Kemonte Fleet is a dynamic individual driven by passion and purpose. A creative force with a keen eye for innovation, Kemonte excels in merging technology. As a lifelong learner, he embraces challenges, weaving a narrative of growth. Kemonte is a catalyst for positive change, leaving an indelible mark.

AFFIRMATION

I am a resilient soul, navigating the tapestry of life. In moments of challenge, I embrace my narrative, knowing each thread contributes to my growth. I choose gratitude, rekindling joy in small moments. Surrounded by support and fueled by faith, I am on a sacred journey of renewal, restoring joy within.

Khyeema Fleet

Khyeema Fleet is a proud mother of one son Samir who pursued her dreams and graduated from Westlake High School with aspiring dreams to become a skilled Cosmetologist, She is a two-time best-selling author.

AFFIRMATION

I am reconnecting with the wellspring of joy that resides within my heart. My inner joy is a constant source of light, and I embrace it once more. I find my way back to the enduring joy that is a part of my true self.

Myairah Fongsue

My name is Myairah Fongsue. I was born in Livingston, New Jersey, and raised in the "Keystone State Philadelphia, Pennsylvania. I am twelve years old. I attended St. Martin Deporres Catholic School, and I currently do online schooling. I learned to swim at a young age. I also did gymnastics. I received ribbons for swimming, and medals for gymnastics. I currently do ballet.

AFFIRMATION

I AM Pretty, I AM Intelligent
I AM Productive. I AM a straight 'A' student.
I AM on time. I have a great attention span.
I AM Helpful. I AM Strong
I AM Motivated. I AM Kind
I AM well put together.
I AM Me; I AM a child of God.

Karen Foote

Karen Foote is a Minister, Author, and Certified Christian Life Coach. Her mission is to help Christian women heal from past hurts and traumas using biblical principles. She is the founder of He Restores My Soul, a ministry that facilitates the healing process. She can be reached on Facebook and Instagram.

AFFIRMATION

I believe in God; He will do what He says He will do. I am who He says I am according to His word in Psalm 139. I can do what He says I can do according to His Word in Philippians 4:13. I believe in God!

Darkema Freeman

My name is Darkema Freeman. I am a mother and grandmother and a prayer warrior. I find Joy in Jesus Christ, my Lord and Savior! I work for a moving company as a Driver, and I love to cook. Preparing family meals is my favorite pastime. I am hoping to open my business, K Cooks, in 2024. I can be found on FB as Darkema

AFFIRMATION

I walk by faith and not by sight therefore I hold tenaciously to the truth that God's word cannot fail. I am conscious of listening to God's Spirit guide me into obedience to God's principles for my benefit.

Sakinah Nacole Freeman

Sakinah Nacole Freeman is a Licensed Social Worker and Certified Grief Counselor. She is the co-author of *Joy Comes in the Morning and In His Presence.*

Website: https://healingheartsmindandsoul.org
Email@info@healingheartsmindandsoul.org

AFFIRMATION

The joy of the lord is my companion on this journey, and I share it generously with others. I embrace each day with gratitude, finding joy in the simple moments of life. I release the past with gratitude and look to the future with hope, anticipating the joy it holds.

Tyquan Freeman

Tyquan Freeman is an aspiring barber dedicated to the art of hair craft. Passionate about creating sharp styles, boosting confidence, and crafting unique looks. He is committed to continuous learning and transforming hair into works of art.

AFFIRMATION

Perform acts of Kindness for others, whether it is helping a neighbor, or participating in a program, or simply offering a kind word. Helping others can bring a profound sense of purpose and Joy.

Rosalie Funderburk

My name is Rosalie Funderburk, I'm a mother of (2) with a bachelor's and master's degree. I was inspired through my children to write poetry and my love continues to grow as I listen to the melodies of my heart towards the Father.
I pray you're blessed through my poem.

AFFIRMATION

Proverbs 3:5-6
Trust in the Lord with all your heart
and lean not on your own understanding.
in all your ways submit to him,
and he will make your paths straight.

Tarshia Galloway

Tarshia Galloway is an Educator, Prophetic liturgical dance minister & teacher, Massage Therapist, wife, mother of 4, and Co-Author. Connect with her on Facebook (Tarshia Galloway) and Instagram as thebeautifulqueentee, dusicmance, tk.royalchainsofarmor

AFFIRMATION

Romans 8:28 NIV
And we know that in all things God works for the good of those who love him, who have been called according to his purpose.

Catrina Garcia

Catrina Garcia, 17-years-old from Florida. I am passionate about playing volleyball and using my talents to glorify Him. You can find me on Instagram @catrina.garcia.volleyball.2024!

AFFIRMATION

I was made fearfully and wonderfully for Your glory. You intricately wove my being, aligning it with the purpose you have ordained for the life you've granted me. You've blessed me with a sound to sing your glory and a temple to position myself toward you.

Toni Garnett

Toni is a retired Army Captain and the founder and CEO of Veteran Force Industries, (VFI). Toni has a strong passion for bridging the gap of employment from military to civilian service for Veterans and their spouses. Connect with her on Facebook at Toni Faithfull and @www.veteranforceinc.com.

AFFIRMATION

When everything feels like an uphill struggle, I just think of the view from the top.

Abidemi Gboluwaga

My name is Abidemi Gboluwaga. I was born in Lagos, Nigeria where I spent much of my adolescent years, before emigrating to Germany.

I am currently a Nursing student, working smart, not hard, to become a great nurse equipped to promote healthy living and to save lives. I chose this vocation to advance the well-being of humanity.

AFFIRMATION

I AM grateful for the gifts of JOY.
I AM a magnet for JOY.
I speak JOY in every situation.
I radiate JOY through my beautiful smile.
JOY keeps me fit and healthy.
I have JOYOUS people around me.
I've got more than enough JOY to share around the world.
God in me is my inner JOY.

Laurie Governor Curtis

Laurie G. Curtis is a leader, motivational speaker, coach, and author. She is a quiet force who speaks out loud, to motivate, and share wisdom and lessons learned. Contact Laurie via email (info@lauriegcurtis.com), website (lauriegcurtis.com) or Facebook (laurie governor curtis)

AFFIRMATION

My gifts and talents are not for me alone but are given to me to fulfill a greater purpose. I am committed to sharing them with others so that God's plan and purpose will be fulfilled!

Sarah Gillet Couto

Sarah Gillet Couto is a wife, mother, and the founder of Gillet Couto Consulting. As an international leadership coach, she specializes in coaching individuals and developing high-performing leadership teams. In 2021 Sarah surrendered her life to Christ...

Contact Information:
coaching@sgilletcouto.com | www.sgilletcouto.com
sarah@sarah4yahweh.com | sarah4yahweh.com
https://www.facebook.com/Sgccoaching
https://www.linkedin.com/in/sarahgilletcouto/
https://www.instagram.com/gilletcoutoconsulting/

AFFIRMATION

I declare Jesus is my only pathway to Joy! I have surrendered to you, my Lord, and I worship you because you are good, and your mercies endure forever. Your word is a lamp to my feet and a light to my path. I always rejoice and pray without ceasing.

____

____

____

____

____

____

____

Tekhari Ghee

Mr. Tekhari A. Ghee is a 2023 high school graduate, debut author (Joy 365), and son of co-author, Dr. Radiance Rose. This fall, he embarks on a new journey at college, channeling his innate curiosity into the realm of engineering, driven by his desire to bring innovation to the world.

AFFIRMATION

I overcome adversity, embrace new beginnings, & unlimited opportunities. Empowered, I unleash my potential and transform dreams into reality.

Patricia Tremble Gilchrist

Patricia Tremble Gilchrist is an educator, ordained minister, poet/author, exhorter, and prayer call host. I am a graduate of Statesboro High School; I received a B.S. in Business Adm. and a Teacher's certification from Paine College. I spend my time doing outreach, hosting my Friday noon, praise, prayer, and worship call, exhorting the people in the house of God, and writing poetry by inspiration of the Holy Spirit, as well as sharing and reciting them occasionally.

AFFIRMATION

I choose to maintain my joy by releasing all negative thoughts and feelings. I count it all joy when I go through tests and trials because the joy of the Lord is my strength.

Dr. Antoria Gillon

Dr. Antoria Gillon has dedicated her life to making a difference in the lives of those who have experienced domestic violence. Driven by her background in psychology. Her unwavering commitment to her mission has enabled her clients to attain stability and self-sufficiency, transforming ordinary lives into extraordinary ones.

AFFIRMATION

Today is a new day. I must release my attachment to the "how" and embrace new possibilities. I am grateful for a fresh start to create new ideas. I permit myself to greet "self" before I meet anyone else.

Sanerica Gipson

Sanerica Gipson is passionate about helping women discover their identity and worth in Christ and be set free from the bondage and lies of the enemy. She is a minister of the Gospel, life coach, author, and founder of Flawed Worthy Free.
Connect with her at www.sanericagipson.com.

AFFIRMATION

With joy set before me, I will endure challenges, disregarding shame, and I will thrive in my purpose. As Jesus sits at God's right hand, I declare that I too will find strength, overcome obstacles, and fulfill my divine destiny.

April Green

April Green is a wife, mother of three children living with Autism Spectrum Disorder, and licensed minister. April has worked in the field of early childhood special education for over 20 years, is a published author, and is currently pursuing her doctorate in educational leadership. April has a passion for promoting autism awareness and early intervention services. April strongly believes that awareness is key to acceptance and is dedicated to being a vehicle for change while helping others find peace and purpose through pain.

AFFIRMATION

I stand in great expectation of the Holy Spirit and the Power of Prayer

Marilyn Green

Was built in East St. Louis, IL. and is the host and producer of her podcast, "Girl, Who Don't You Know?!" on Facebook and YouTube. She is one of the co-authors in, "Stuck is Not Your Story! I Overcame and Am Victorious".
Contact her @ aheartthatisbrave@gmail.com

AFFIRMATION

I am joyful in the morning and the evening.
I am receiving the strength that God promised me because I am joyful.
I rejoice in Him all day.
I show God in me every day.
I know that Jesus loves me.
I am a friend of God.

Tiffany Green

Tiffany, a trailblazer in the literary industry and the mastermind behind TA MEDIA CO, has been relentlessly supporting authors since 2007. With her relentless drive, she has successfully elevated numerous authors to new heights, fostering their creativity and expanding their income streams through a myriad of innovative services. www.publishwithtiffany.com

AFFIRMATION

Embrace life's radiant moments, one day at a time. Find your joy in every sunrise, painting each day with vibrant hues of happiness.

Nicole Gribstad

Nicole Gribstad is a Best Selling Author, Motivational Speaker, Practical Bible Application, Deliverance Mindset Minister, and Homeschool/Parent Wellness Advisor. Nicole equips motivated Christian professionals to break free from feeling overwhelmed, confused, stressed, and anxiety to proclaim purpose clarity and achieve fun, fitness, freedom, and fulfillment in life and business.

AFFIRMATION

I delightfully receive Christ's abundant blessing riches! God's dreams and heavenward destinations are for me. I recognize what God wants me to see and learn in every situation. I make masterpieces as I believe and walk intimately in His Holy Presence. His truth and worship are always on my lips!

Deborah A. Griffiths

Deborah A. Griffiths was born and raised in the greater Los Angeles area. She graduated from Biola University with honors earning a Bachelor of Science degree in Organizational Leadership. Her published works include "Torched – Burnt by a Gaslighter" to bring awareness on gaslighting and domestic abuse. She is the proud mother of three grown children and considers her faith and family most important.

Website: www.brokentoboldness.com
Instagram – debbiegriffiths581 | Facebook debbie.griffiths.77
LinkedIn – debbie-griffiths-43b1291a | Twitter - @cidmgr7

AFFIRMATION

"And you will know the truth, and the truth will set you free." John 8:32 ESV

____
____
____
____
____
____
____
____
____
____

Challon Hall

Challon Hall: I was born and currently reside in Maryland and lived in Hampton Virginia for approximately 10+ years between 2001-2017. I am an entrepreneur of many traits. I have 2 sons named Karson (16) and Ammon II "Deuce" (5). I enjoy laughter and the joys of living my life to the fullest.
Social Media: IG @1bella_chacha

AFFIRMATION

Through the pain and suffering I suffered throughout the years; I have vowed to keep GOD first and to always make time for him. I vow to bring comfort and happiness into my life. I vow to not allow anyone to live rent free in my head and to speak on how I feel on any situation needed for my sanity. I vow to give my sons the love and affection I didn't receive growing up and more. I vow to keep speaking positively into my space and people who mean me good into my heart. I vow to BE THE BETTER VERSION OF ME!!

____

____

____

____

____

____

____

____

Celine Hamilton

Celine Hamilton is a Campus Recruiter for a large consulting firm. She is passionate about helping college students navigate through their job search and helping them start their careers.
Connect with her on LinkedIn, https://www.linkedin.com/in/celine-hamilton-225bb6125/

AFFIRMATION

Embrace each day with a heart brimming with gratitude, inviting joy to fill every moment.

Megan M. Hamm

Megan M. Hamm, LPC is the owner of a mental health clinic in Mississippi. She helps individuals and families of all ages to recover from generational trauma. She is an expert in play therapy, trauma, and attachment who specializes in CBT and EMDR. Visit her website at www.meganmhamm.com.

AFFIRMATION

We will increase our skills and faith by focusing on the promises of God. Those promises give us the foundation to prepare for the personal fires of tomorrow. Fire fighters learn to fight fires and believers learn to believe. Believe in God's promises for our life.

Christy Harris

Christy Dawn Harris is an Entrepreneur, Certified Life Coach, and the Owner of Healthy Bizness. She uses her passion to empower others to reach their greatness and unlimited potential. Healthy Bizness is an entrepreneur platform that speaks to the whole person in health, wellness, and beauty. Email: healthybiznesscoach@gmail.com

AFFIRMATION

I choose joy, gratitude, and thankfulness.
I am an overcomer and walk in faith, confidence, and boldness.
I release negative thinking and replace it with positive thoughts. I am filled with peace, happiness, and love.
I am transformed through the renewal of my mind daily.
I am blessed and will bless others.

Joy Harris

My name is Joy Harris, born and raised in the rural community of Aboukir, in St. Ann, Jamaica West Indies. I am the eighth of eleven children, and I was known for special abilities in drama. I studied Hospitality Management in Jamaica, and I became a Healthcare Specialist here in the USA.
I am a Christian, winning souls for Christ.
http://www.jamaicaglory.com

AFFIRMATION

I choose a path of wellness and success.
I begin each day with a grateful heart.
I AM pure positive energy.
Limitless JOY is my birthright.
JOY is the essence of my being.
I AM who God says I am.
I AM worthy and deserving of a lifetime filled with happiness and JOY.

Marshelle Harris

Marshelle Harris Founder of Wellness 4 Life, passionate about helping women to achieve optimal health without feeling hungry, stressed, or overwhelmed after a diagnosis. She is a Paid and Published Author, *Cancer Won't Stop Me*, helping women unleash the power within to become unstoppable.
lintr.ee/marshelleharris | www.marshelleharris.com

AFFIRMATION

I will seek the guidance of the Holy Spirit to cultivate patience, kindness, humility, and forgiveness in my relationships. I will rely on God's unending love, God's love, never fails. May His love shine through me and draw others closer to the heart of our loving Father.

Yonder Harrison

Yonder
www.yonderpresents.com

AFFIRMATION

I release all negative thoughts and emotions, and inhale positivity, peace, and gratitude. I trust in my abilities and know that everything will work out for my highest good. I am centered, focused, and ready to face any challenge with clarity and composure. I am capable, worthy, and deserving of all the good that comes my way. I am grateful for this moment and the opportunity to live my best life.

Tiffany Harvey

Tiffany Harvey is a Naval Officer, Chief of Acquisition at the Department of Interior, and Owner of Pick Your Sweet Poison. Connect with her on Facebook, Instagram and at www.cocktailrecipes.com.

AFFIRMATION

Straighten your crown and hold your head high because you were made strong, fearless, and powerful, and can conquer it all.

Myrrie Hayes

Myrrie Hayes, a successful entrepreneur, started a multimillion-dollar empire in the behavioral industry, providing quality care for the severely mentally ill. With a consulting agency, staffing agency, training academy, and nonprofit, she has achieved remarkable growth, changing lives and inspiring others to replicate her success. You can follow her or get more information at:
https://www.facebook.com/TheMyrrieHayes/
https://www.instagram.com/themyrriehayes/
https://www.youtube.com/@myrrie06/videos

AFFIRMATION

3 affirmations inspired by the Joy restoration devotional:
I am resilient and can overcome any challenges that come my way. I am grateful for the simple pleasures that bring me joy every day. I am a blessing to others, radiating kindness and making a positive impact in their lives.

____

____

____

____

____

____

____

Victoria E. Henderson

Victoria E. Henderson is the host of the internet show, Living Life Victoriously, as well as co-host of Authors Up. She is the author of *When I Need a Word, God Speaks!* with its accompanying journal. Check out her blog at www.victoriaehenderson.com, and on social media @victoriaehenderson.

AFFIRMATION

Today, I choose joy! God gives me joy! I am Joy!
My Name is Joy!

Lorieen D. Henry

Lorieen D. Henry is a servant of God, wife, mother, veteran, published author, podcaster, brand ambassador, and cheerleader of women. Let's connect on Facebook, Instagram, and @www.lorieenhenry.com

AFFIRMATION

I am confident that I will carry out the good work that God has begun in me! Being confident of this, that he who began a good work in you will carry it on to completion until the day of Christ Jesus. Philippians 1:6

Patricia A. Henry

Patricia A. Henry has an immense passion for serving the Lord and exemplifies humility and grace in all that she does. She shared Authorship in the Collaborated book *Joy Comes in the Morning.* As an emerging author, Patricia believes that inspirational messages are God's methods of healing for the soul.

AFFIRMATION

I affirm that I am wearing a crown of beauty in exchange for ashes. My garment is a garment of praise in exchange for heaviness. I affirm that I am anointed with the oil of joy in exchange for sorrow and I am called a tree of righteousness.

Reagan Henry

Reagan Henry is a high school Freshman and a Presidential Scholar who loves reading and is active in her church, school, and community. Look for more from Reagan in the future.

AFFIRMATION

Lord, I can move forward and complete things I have started because of you. I no longer worry about my trials and tribulations. I cast all my cares upon you because your word says, "I Can".

Dr. Serelda L. Herbin, MBA, DSL, CDE

Serelda L. Herbin is the CEO and Founder of Coaching That Cares by Serelda, LLC, a company that coaches current and future leaders from all walks of life, young and old. She is also a published author of two books, *From at Risk To At The Top* and *31 Diversity Thoughts*- both Bestsellers. Connect with her on Facebook, @DrSerelda Ledet Herbin, and at www.coachingthatcares.com

AFFIRMATION

I will speak about what I want to see and work toward it. I will show up daily and walk in my NEXT. Affirming yourself daily feeds your soul. Connect with a higher power and higher mission for yourself. You are worth every second of the day. Go for it!

Judy A. Hewitt

Judy A. Hewitt is a 2x bestselling author, caregiver advocate, and speaker. Hewitt conveys approaching each season of life with faith, hope, and the promise of eternal joy. Titled: *Joy in Every Season: Embracing God's Perfect Timing.*

Connect with Judy
www.Facebook.com/Judy Ann Hewitt
letsconnect@judyahewitt.com

AFFIRMATION

"I trust in God's perfect timing, knowing that each season has a purpose."
"My joy is a gift to be shared with others, creating a ripple of positivity."
"I embrace life's changing seasons with faith, hope, and resilience."
"God's plan unfolds beautifully in every season of my life."

____

____

____

____

____

____

____

____

____

Gwendolyn Hubbard-Harrison

Gwendolyn Hubbard-Harrison is an extraordinary individual, government contracting specialist, author, and money strategist. She had a remarkable career in the Federal government assisting a host of small businesses obtain contracts. Her dedication to safeguarding critical information is unparalleled. As a licensed financial coach, serial entrepreneur, and passionate advocate for upward mobility, Gwendolyn has empowered numerous individuals to achieve their financial goals. With her exceptional intelligence and unwavering commitment, she continues to make a profound impact in both government and business sectors.

AFFIRMATION

I affirm my commitment to embrace healing and renewal.
I can navigate the complexities of grief and allowing joy into my life once again. I embrace opportunities for new memories, and new connections, and explore the beauty still surrounding me.
I grow stronger and more resilient with each step I take.

Teresa Hawley-Howard

Teresa Hawley Howard is a Mother to six beautiful girls, a wife, and a Mimi to her wonderful grandbabies. She is an international best-selling author and publisher. Her passion is helping women find their purpose and their voice. She volunteers with the local domestic violence shelters, and animal shelters and is an advocate for children who have suffered abuse and trauma. She recently graduated with her certification in Mental Health Coaching specializing in Childhood abuse and trauma.
You can connect with her at www.teresahawleyhoward.com

AFFIRMATION

Radiate positivity, allowing your joyful energy to uplift those around you.

Tekesha Hicks

Tekesha Hicks A licensed Minister at the Restoration Church of Daytona. She loves the Lord and has operated in a prophetic dance ministry for over thirteen years. God has allowed her to share that gift with other ministries and that brings her joy. Tekesha obtained a Bachelor of Arts in educational studies with a minor in psychology from Bethune Cookman University. She furthered her education in 2020, at which time she earned a Diploma of Practical Theology from International Seminary, Daytona Beach Satellite Campus. Tekesha has been an early childhood teacher for seventeen years. She enjoys traveling and reading African American Christian Books.

AFFIRMATION

Every hardship that I go through enriches my soul and trust in God.

Yenisen Hidalgo

Yenisen Hidalgo: I am married to a wonderful man and a mother to two children. I'm also a homeschool ESE teacher. This passion for teaching has helped me love studying the word of God. As a result, I now have a passion for teaching the word of God to all ages.
Website: https://thebluelineangels.com/about/yenisen-hidalgo/
Social media: Instagram: learn_with_mrs.yenisen

AFFIRMATION

I will focus on the Lord's blessings in all aspects of my life.
When I'm in the middle of a problem, I will look at it from a positive perspective. The Lord turns my weeping sorrows into joyful praise. I will always praise the Lord.
My joy comes from the Lord.

Andrea L. Hines

Andrea L. Hines A mother, grandmother, author, poet, broadcast host, speaker, and certified life coach is a native of Washington, D.C. now living in Raleigh, NC. She believes her move deepened her relationship with God and lets her creativity flow freely as she shares His words for you. andrealhines.com

AFFIRMATION

I am chosen to shift the atmosphere as the light and love of Christ emanate from me. God gets the glory from His divine appointments when I am obedient. Transformation and restoration occur as weakness becomes strength, hopelessness turns into joy, and my love walk becomes a lifestyle.

Jescika Holloway

Jescika Holloway is a Mother, Wife, Sister, Grandmother, Entrepreneur. I've been married for 27 years. We have 6 children, I have 5 siblings, and 5 grandchildren.
I started my business in 2019 and specialize in custom gourmet pastries. Contact me on Instagram @ Cicis_sweetsand treats. Glory be to God!

AFFIRMATION

So, to affirm all that I have shared with you, I am a miracle on assignment to touch lives through my testimony. You can do anything you put your hands to. With God's help. Don't be afraid to just jump and take a risk, a world changer, someone who will simply say" Yes Lord."

Lisa T. Horton

Lisa T. Horton Christian Relationship Coach and Speaker Lisa's expertise lies in guiding individuals to have healthier relationships by building confidence, setting healthy boundaries, confronting fears, and loving yourself. This is the beginning of a positive transformation. Lisa has 7 years of Coaching Experience. Lisa earned her certificates from World Coaching Institute and HIScoach Training Academy
www.2yourheartlifecoaching.com www.amazon.com/author/lisahorton
Facebook- LisaLisa-Author

AFFIRMATION

Repentance Prayer
Dear Lord, Thank you for your forgiveness and grace.
Thank you for not abandoning me in my mistakes.
Help me to welcome advice, rather than criticism.
Help me to build rather than destroy. Thank you for offering me humility and guidance as I continue to read your Word.

Francine Houston

Francine Houston is a graphic and fashion designer, poet, and published author. www.francinehouston.com.

AFFIRMATION

The joy of the Lord is my strength.
I lean on God in times of grief.
God is my comforter and strength.
I will sing songs of praise and worship unto God and stay full of joy.

Lorinda Hawkins Smith, MBA

Lorinda Hawkins Smith is the author of the book and solo play series: *Justice? Or… Just Me?* She is an actor, advocate, comedian, musician, domestic violence survivor, and more. Lorinda earned her MBA while transitioning from houseless to housed. Connect with her on Facebook, Instagram, TikTok, and at lorindahawkinssmith.com

AFFIRMATION

I am not a mistake. My life has a purpose. I will walk in my calling. I am not an accident. God had me in mind before the foundations of the world. I am a walking miracle. I will use my gifts to bless others. My best days are ahead of me.

Choose Joy

Joy Hutchinson

I am Joyan Hutchinson. I am from the parish of Manchester in Jamaica West Indies. I am the seventh of ten children. I attended St. Andrew Technical High School doing Commercial Studies.
I worked in the USA as a Nursing Assistant. I am the mom of six beautiful children and six beautiful grandchildren. I love God. He is my everything.
Joyh20209@gmail.com

AFFIRMATION

I AM Healthy and I AM Strong. When I look at my past, I only see my accomplishments. I do not see failures.
My mind is a magnet for abundance and peace, success flows effortlessly into my life. I trust in the Lord, and HE works wonders in my life.
I AM vivacious, happy, and sociable.

Deborah Ivey

Deborah Ivey is the author of Overcoming the Odds and My New Bold Journal: A Woman's Path to Showing Up Boldy for Christ. She has coauthored 5 books *Tapping into Your Inner Beauty, Daily Devotional II., Your Wings Were Ready but My Heart Was Not, I Told the Storm, and Finding Joy in Your Journey Devotional*. Deborah has taken Women's Empowerment Coach, Certified Leadership Coach, Certified Professional Speakers, and Certified International Entrepreneur Coach Certifications through the Professional Woman's Network. Deborah is a Certified Life Coach, Certified Pre-Marital and Marriage Coach Hiscoach, and Christian Lifecoach.

AFFIRMATION

I Am Worthy of all good things coming my way. You do not determine my worth.

Charlotte Izzard

Charlotte Izzard is a Diversity, Equity, Inclusion, and Accessibility (DEIA), Team Building Strategist and the founder of Grow on Another Level (G.o.A.L). Charlotte believes in creating a common language within organizational cultures, working as a catalyst to break through the barriers of stereotyping or pigeonholing people, and helping to highlight inclusivity.

AFFIRMATION

Don't wonder when the merry-go-round is going to stop - get off, change directions, and trust God.

LaShonda Jack

LaShonda Jack: I Am Beauty.

AFFIRMATION

I Am Beauty, I Am Worthy, I Am Exceptional, I Am Authentic, I Am Whole, I Am Introspective, I Am Peaceful, I Am Divine, I Am Magnetic, I Am Resourceful, I Am Abundant, I Am Wisdom Exemplified, I Am Forgiving, I Am Loyal, I Am God's Magnum Opus.

Dr. Maisha L. Jack

Dr. Maisha L. Jack is an international speaker, international best-selling author, business owner, coach, and self-publisher. Dr. Jack, also a wife, mother, and grandmother, has been a dual-certified educator and leader in general and special education for 20+ years. For more information, call 404-610-1506 or visit Maishajack.com, linkedin.com/in/maisha-jack https://www.instagram.com/thehoneybuttercompanybooks/ https://m.facebook.com/pages/category/Product-Service/The-Honey-Butter-Book-Company-

AFFIRMATION

Father God,
I thank you for guiding and supporting me in all that I do. At this next juncture in my life, I will be strong and courageous. I will be unafraid, and I will be encouraged, for YOU, my LORD, and my GOD, will be with me wherever I go.

Queen Jackie

Queen JackieA is a Holistic Life/Intimacy Coach! My journey as a life coach began in 2010 while working as a Masseuse! In 2019 I was a guest on The Today Show, and a few months later I won an EXPY AWARD through leaders and coaches! In 2017, I created Intimate Connections which is a popular podcast. You can follow me on Instagram @queen_jackiea.

AFFIRMATION

Intimately Connected
I radiate light because I'm intimately connected to myself.
I'm a masterpiece and there's no one like me because I'm unique!
I manifest success in all areas of my life because I deserve it.
I invest in my dreams because I'm worthy of success.
I am the author of my story, and each day another great chapter is written.

____

____

____

____

____

____

____

____

Choose Joy

Karen Jackson

I'm Karen M. Jackson. I live in Flora, Ms. I grew up in Los Angeles. I'm a widow with two beautiful daughters and three amazing grandchildren. I've been Employed at East Flora School for 26 years where this is more than just a job, it's my assignment from God.

AFFIRMATION

We often do life with our heads down, allow me to encourage you to hold your head up. Why, you say? Because our all-knowing God has so much more for you. And you need to be able to see it when it comes your way. Now look up!

Mirta I. Jackson

Mirta I. Jackson is a Human Resource professional and holds a Master of Professional Studies with an advanced study in Human Resources and Employment Relations with an emphasis in Ethics and Leadership from Pennsylvania State University (PSU). She is Lifetime member for many groups. You can reach her at the below:

Facebook: Quentin-Mirta Jackson
Facebook Page: Books'n'Vibes
Business Site: JVG Inc.
Email: mirta.jackson@yahoo.com

AFFIRMATION

I am grateful to get out of bed, see my family, and to share my love with others. Every day will be a great day with moments of joy and happiness. Every day is my day!

Shawne Jackson

Shawne Jackson, a visionary entrepreneur, and community advocate, is the driving force behind successful startups. With a keen sense of social impact, Shawne leads with innovation. Discover more at www.shamonjgifts.com and engage on Facebook at www.facebook.com/shawnej.
Committed to positive change, Shawne empowers communities through leadership.

AFFIRMATION

I embrace each day with gratitude, radiating joy and sharing love, knowing that God's blessings are abundant, and His presence is my constant source of strength.

Rev. Dr. Patricia Ann Johnson Dowtin

Rev. Dr. Patricia Ann Johnson Dowtin Born & raised in Washington DC Married the late Joseph T. Dowtin, Jr. Mother of Monique Morton, Unique Dowtin, and grandmother of Joshua Morton. “If I can help somebody as I travel along, then my living shall not be in vain.” email: 1pa.johnsondowtin@gmail.com

AFFIRMATION

Embrace each day with a heart brimming with gratitude, inviting joy to fill every moment.

J. "MsChardae Jennings

J. "MsChardae Jennings Born and raised in Chicago, Illinois, Joyce Jennings is a US Navy Veteran. She attended Northern Illinois University but graduated from DeVry, Chicago, with a Bachelor's degree in Computer Information Systems. Currently resides in Atlanta, Georgia with her two children.
www.MsChardae.com website
whiskersbrew86@yahoo.com email

AFFIRMATION

It is better to be rejected by someone or something not meant for you than accepted by something or someone that means you are no good. Never take advice from people who have never been where you are trying to go.

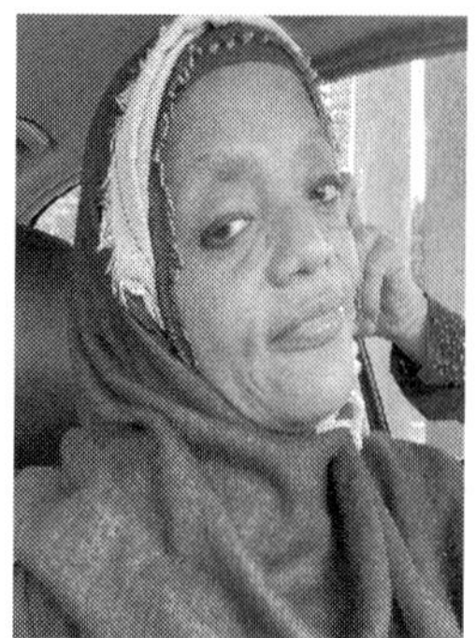

Lakeisha Jennings

Lakeisha Jennings is a proud graduate of Orange High School. She is a driven and accomplished individual with a passion for lifelong learning and personal growth. Lakeisha's educational journey is just the beginning of her story, and she looks forward to making a positive impact on the world.

AFFIRMATION

I am a resilient soul, capable of restoring joy in my life. I embrace self-compassion, finding strength in my imperfections. Through gratitude and forgiveness, I release the past's burdens, making way for joy's return. I am the master of my happiness, and I welcome it with open arms.

Choose Joy

Nathan Jennings Jr.

Nathan Jennings is a Jr. Passionate barber shop owner with a flair for timeless styles. He is dedicated to crafting personalized grooming experiences that leave clients not just looking but feeling their best. He is a tastemaker in the art of barbering, creating a welcoming haven for both tradition and trend.

AFFIRMATION

In the tapestry of life, I am the artisan of my joy. Through every clip and conversation, I shape not just hair but a canvas of positivity. I am a beacon of light, restoring joy in every stroke. Today, I affirm my power to uplift and transform lives through my craft.

Tasha Jennings

Tasha Jennings is an Insurance Specialist Supervisor for Behavioral Health. I absolutely love what I do. I am a Mom and a Gigi of two wonderful granddaughters, Big Sister and loving Auntie, living my best life. You can find me on fb as Tasha Jennings.

AFFIRMATION

I have joy like a river that never runs dry. My heart is constantly full of Joy, and it spreads through everything I do. Everything I touch becomes gold because I do what I do from a place of joy. I am joyful and I spread joy!

Heidi Jensen

Heidi Jensen (M.Ed. TESOL) is an author, educator, missionary, and language communications coach. Since 1997, she has been serving members of the United Nations community, often developing faith-based materials to begin spiritual conversations among ethnically, culturally, and spiritually diverse groups.
Connect with her on Facebook or via email:
Heidi@HeidiLynnJensen.com

AFFIRMATION

Although you can't choose your circumstances, you can choose your response. Choose thankfulness and joy because God chose YOU and He has chosen to walk with you through each of those circumstances. He has an adventure ahead and blessings He can't wait to bring into your life!

Deborah Juniper-Frye

Deborah Juniper-Frye, Grief Care Consulting, Owner; Grief Recovery Method Specialist; 23 Years of Grief Experience and Expertise; Life & Recovery Coach; Amazon Best Selling Author 11X's; Global Conference Speaker, and a Contributing Writer for OWN IT Magazine. My website is www.griefcareconsulting.com and my email address is dfrye.gcc@gmail.com.
Instagram @griefcareconsulting
Facebook @ Deborah Frye
Twitter @GriefCConsult
LinkedIn @ Deborah Frye

AFFIRMATION

"Take advantage of the new GRACE and MERCY. Let Him refresh your mind, body, and soul with His Amazing Love. And remember, you are able to Endure, Overcome, and Begin Again with hope, purpose, and uncovered faith." Deborah Juniper-Frye

____
____
____
____
____
____
____
____

Zontayvia Solomon Jiles

Zontayvia Solomon Jiles is a Georgia native. She has earned her master's in business administration. Emphasizing in healthcare management. Mrs. Solomon Jiles currently holds the position of Patient Safety Manager at a local military treatment facility, the owner of WriteWay, LLC, and the co- founder of Worthy Youth Community Outreach.

Ways to Stay Connected:
Email: writeway19@gmail.com
Phone: 229-800-5422
https://worthyyouthoutreach.com

AFFIRMATION

Today and all day I am filled with gratitude and greatness.
Today and every day I will make the right choices by using the inner light. I will shine the light that is within me for others to see.

____

____

____

____

____

____

____

____

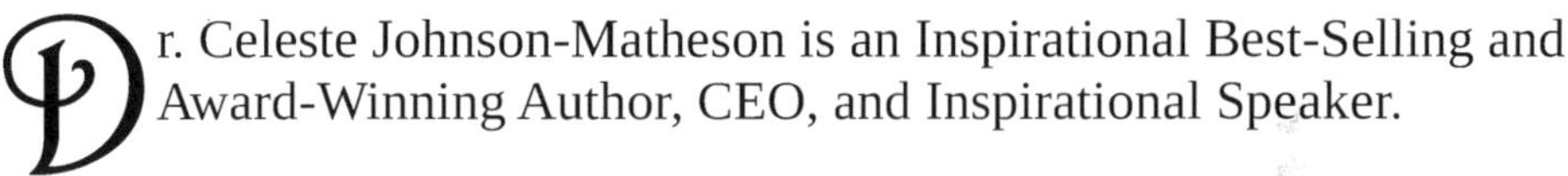

Dr. Celeste Johnson-Matheson

Dr. Celeste Johnson-Matheson is an Inspirational Best-Selling and Award-Winning Author, CEO, and Inspirational Speaker.

AFFIRMATION

"Consider it pure joy, my brothers, and sisters, whenever you face trials of many kinds, because you know that the testing of your faith produces perseverance. Let perseverance finish its work so that you may be mature and complete, not lacking anything." James 1:2-4

Alexandria Evelyn Johnson

Alexandria Evelyn Johnson is a trained Clinical Psychologist and Child Forensic Specialist, an ordained Youth Pastor, an international speaker, and a published author. She enjoys helping others live optimally and passionately from the inside out. Connect with her on Facebook at Salt and Light International or via email at saltandlightweare@gmail.com.

AFFIRMATION

I acknowledge that joy is my weapon of power to get me through seasons of suffering. I activate my joy now. I am filled with joy. I am overflowing with joy. I will ensure that my joy tank is never empty.

Lakeisha Johnson

My name is Lakeisha Johnson. I am an Overcomer! I am a victim of molestation, rape and domestic violence. That does not define 'who' or rather I say 'whose' I am. I find Joy in Jesus Christ, my Lord and savior! I am the owner of Blessings of Overcoming, a non-profit organization that helps women overcome the obstacles that occur in life.

AFFIRMATION

I embrace joy in every moment, finding happiness in the simple and the extraordinary.

Michelle Johnson

Michelle Johnson, a native of Dallas/Fort Worth, Texas, is a REALTOR® with a passion for real estate and has vast industry experience. She is also a dedicated mother who enjoys reading, traveling, and investing in real estate.https://www.michellejrealtor.com

AFFIRMATION

I effortlessly attract love, happiness, and all life's good things. My confidence, intuition, and gratitude guide me toward success, abundance, and positivity. I conquer challenges with grace and determination, surrounded by love and support. I am enough, embracing my unique qualities and eagerly anticipating a bright future.

Norma Johnson

My name is Norma Johnson, originally from Jamaica, migrated to the USA in 2001. Wife, Mother, Entrepreneur. I love helping people whether, be Health Wealth, or just plain happiness by way of Motivation and /or Inspiration that the Holy Spirit granted me as a Gift and Talent.

AFFIRMATION

I am Peaceful, Happy, Healthy, Abundant, Worthy, Grateful, Confident, Courageous. I am manifesting through prayers and waiting patiently for the answers while I do the work to accomplish them. I live in the Richness and peace that God given me in my spirit before I was born.

Dr. Sasha Johnson

Dr. Sasha Johnson is from Montgomery, Alabama. She is a counselor, author, professor, and speaker. She founded a nonprofit organization called Sister's 2nd Chance and Inside and Out Consulting, a mental health private practice. She has her Doctorate Degree in Psychology. She is a professor at Yorkville and California Universities.

Social Media Handles:

IG: www.instagram.com/drsashamercedes
FB: www.facebook.com/drsashamercedes
Twitter: www.twitter.com/drsashamercedes
Linkedin: www.linkedin.com/drsashajohnson
Website: www.drsashamercedes.com

AFFIRMATION

Joy comes when you find peace and gratitude in the difficult moments that attack your life.

____

____

____

____

____

____

____

____

Pastor Janice Stepney Jones

A believer in Jesus Christ. Pastor Jones has encouraged and worked with many on their journey. Offering guidance and inspiring people to seek a deeper relationship with Jesus. Pastor Janice has a passion for empowering people from all different walks of life. She's a one-time Author of *Voice of Hope*, certified motivational speaker, and leader of a Pastoral committee, and she attends Vinings Church in Smyrna Georgia.

AFFIRMATION

Heavenly Father, thank you for making your plan clear. My heart and mind are open to the promises of your word. You're able to speak to your people individually, experiencing the secret place where there are no eyes or ears but You alone. I pour out my spirit to You. In Jesus Name Amen.

Roe Jones

Roe Jones is a Senior Vice President in Technology for the one of largest banks in the US, an entrepreneur who founded multiple businesses, a real estate investor, and a two-time best-selling author. Connect with her on Clubhouse/Instagram @RoeJonology or LinkedIn.

AFFIRMATION

"But my God shall supply all your needs according to his riches in glory by Christ Jesus." Philippians 4:19

Theresa Jordan

Theresa Jordan resides in Orlando, Florida. For additional information email Triumphantmagazine2017@gmail.com. and amothersheart2023@gmail.com

AFFIRMATION

Embrace change as an opportunity for growth, inviting newfound joy into your evolving life.

Patricia Ann Bean-Kane

Patricia Ann Bean- Kane is a writer, actress, and Director of Christian Elite Ensemble and Love in Action, an outreach ministry. Patricia is employed with the Equal Employment Opportunity Commission as an Enforcement Manager.

AFFIRMATION

Let your inner child play, igniting the spark of joy that resides within you.

Cheryl Kehl

Cheryl Kehl is an author, cleric, business generalist, and a faith-based family coach, with a heart for broken women and domestic violence victims. Moved deeply by her faith in God, Cheryl is a certified Christian life coach. in the business of seeing women reinstate healthy boundaries rooted in a relationship with Christ.

AFFIRMATION

God has given this day and therefore, I will rejoice and be glad in it. "This is the day the LORD has made; I will rejoice and be glad in it." (Psalm 118:64, ESV)

Reneisha Kennedy

Reneisha is the author of the “Motivating Your Morning” devotional. She holds 2 degrees in Early Childhood & Family Education. She is a licensed finance coach and life coach. She’s a woman who loves God!!

Keep in touch with her:
Website: www.reneishakennedy.com
Email: generationwealth22@gmail.com
Fb: RK Coaching Services/Neisha Kayy
Instagram: rkcoachings

AFFIRMATION

You are filled with the joy of the Lord. You are fearfully & wonderfully made. You are more than a conqueror. You are the head & not the tail. Seeing yourself how God sees you will give you the joy & peace you long for!!

____

____

____

____

____

____

____

____

Althea King

Althea King is a Licensed Mental Health Counselor. Author Althea tailors her client-centered counseling style to enhance the client's level of motivation for personal growth and Divine transformation. Connect with Althea on Facebook.

AFFIRMATION

Unveiled

"But we all, with unveiled face, beholding as in a mirror the glory of the Lord, are being transformed into the same image from glory to glory, just as from the Lord, the Spirit." *2 Corinthians 3:18*

Today I Choose to Take Off Masks I Wear to Protect Me…

Elder Kimberly King

Elder Kimberly King is an educator for Department of Defense Schools, currently residing in Vilseck, Germany. She is ordained as an Evangelist/Pastor and has served in various areas of ministry. She is currently serving and ministering at New Life Christian Center in Vilseck, Germany. kingkimberly954@gmail.com

AFFIRMATION

I speak into each day and declare that it will cooperate with God's plans. Anything sent to frustrate your purposes for each day is bound now, in Jesus' name. I declare that today is pregnant with a purpose that will propel me towards my destiny.

Lindsay Kinslow

Lindsay is a retired veteran of the US Army, best-selling author, business owner, and corporate trainer with over 20 years of management experience. She is dedicated to giving back to her community and empowering veterans, and young adults.
More about her at www.lindsaykinslow.com.

AFFIRMATION

"I am an embodiment of unstoppable resilience, capable of rising above any challenge or adversity with unwavering strength and perseverance."

Alicia Kirschner

Alicia Kirschner is a lover of the word of YHWH and grounded in Yeshua. She teaches the word to all ages, is dedicated to the saving of souls through Yeshua, and seeks to use her gifts to bless the kingdom. She is an entrepreneur and blessed mother of 3.

AFFIRMATION

Our Minds Are Doors to Our Spirit.
Transform anxiety into peace and joy daily renewing your mind. Romans 12:2. Commit to memorizing verses about anxiety. This will equip you for that moment when anxiety comes knocking. Remember not all who knock at your door need to enter your mind gate.

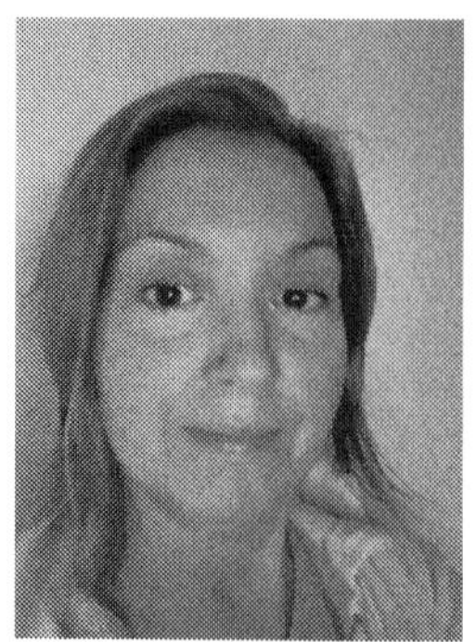

Christina Krausslach

With a B.S. in Psychology and a B.S. in Administration of Justice, she encourages others to enjoy the study of God's Word with real joy. As ordained and an intercessor, enveloping study with prayer is also a joy shared here with this devotional.

AFFIRMATION

I am filled with the Holy Spirit. I am singing and making melodies to the Lord in my heart. I am giving thanks in the name of Jesus Christ for God's rejoicing over me with singing. I am a worshiper in spirit and truth. I am His.

Dr. A'Londa L. Kusimo

Dr. A'Londa L. Barber-Kusimo is an acclaimed, international best-selling author of 5 books. Her work has been featured in several publications. She also runs her own business as a graphic designer and Brandologist. Dr. ABKusimo has been a keynote speaker and presenter at various events.

She can be reached at:
Website: www.ABKusimo.com
Email: ALondaLKusimo@gmail.com

AFFIRMATION

I thank you Father for making my life a bundle of joy and happiness. Your joy in my heart is my strength, and with joy, I draw out prosperity, peace, success, health, and other blessings from deep within me today, in Jesus' Name. Amen.

Emmanuel O. Kusimo

Emmanuel Olorunsola Kusimo is God's Servant, an Engineer, and an aspiring author. He has always had a passion for writing and has been writing Christian devotionals in his spare time. Emmanuel brings a unique perspective to his work as an engineer in his profession.
He can be reached at:
Email: EmmanuelKusimo2022@gmail.com

AFFIRMATION

The Lord Jesus, through His vicarious death and triumphant resurrection, has brought me into a life of unlimited joy, victory, dominion, and righteousness. Therefore, I rejoice evermore, with joy unspeakable, and full of glory. My joy is of the Holy Ghost, and it knows no bounds. Hallelujah!

____
____
____
____
____
____
____
____
____

Almeria Lacy

Almeria Lacy is a Minister with a love for sharing God's gospel. She is a retired combat Veteran, co-founder of Sigma Phi Psi Military Sorority, Inc., Rotarian, and CEO of Crime and Self Protection Awareness Advisors. She was born in LA but resides in Houston, TX. She is on IG as GiDimples and FB as Almeria Lacy.

AFFIRMATION

"I am a child of our Heavenly Father; His love for me is immeasurable."

Marnie Lacy

Allow me to introduce myself, my name is Marnie Lacy, mother, grandmother, best-selling co-author, and a child of God. I hold an AAS in Early Childhood Development

AFFIRMATION

Dance through life's challenges with grace, knowing that joy is your constant companion.

Latonya Lamb

Latonya Reed-Lamb is a retired Army Veteran, Security Professional, Ministry Leader, Mentor, and Mother. She holds a Master of Science in Critical Incident Management from St. Leo University, a Bachelor of Science in Criminal Justice Administration from Park University, and a Chief Diversity and Inclusion Officer Certificate from George Mason University.
Connect with author Latonya Reed-Lamb at just_latonya_b on Instagram

AFFIRMATION

John 16:33, In this world you will have trouble. But take heart! I have overcome the world.

____

____

____

____

____

____

____

____

____

____

____

Daniel E. Landrum

Daniel E. Landrum was born in Atlanta, GA and is a veteran of the United States Army. During his twenty-year Army career and five deployments, he used his gifts of song and words of encouragement to keep all around him trusting and believing in the Lord.

AFFIRMATION

I'm a child of God; I am who God says I am not who the world says I am. No matter what comes my way my joy will never fade because the Lord God Almighty gave it to me and I won't let the world take it away from me.

Mohogani Lattie

Mohogani is a proud graduate of Hillsboro High School, where she excelled in academics and made lasting memories. Her high school journey equipped her with the skills and determination to pursue her dreams, and she continues to shine in her post-graduation endeavors.

AFFIRMATION

"I cultivate hope and joy in every expectation I hold. The future is bright, and I look forward to it with a joyful heart. My expectations are filled with the promise of joy."

Adrianah Marie Lewis

My name is Adrianah Marie Lewis. I'm 12 years old and going to the 7th grade. I live in Killeen, Texas. I am the 3rd youngest of 4. Some hobbies I enjoy outside of school are cheerleading, praise dancing, helping with my mom's daycare, and one of my favorite subjects is reading.

AFFIRMATION

I'm thankful for my life and what God has to offer for many years to come. As blessings come through take them and use them, for uplifting. When I grow up, I want to go to college and have a major in the medical field.

Dr. Tina D. Lewis

Dr. Tina D. Lewis, known as The Bottom-Line Queen, is a Global Business Strategist and Founder of Global Women Speakers who positions you to share your Message, Products and Services around the World!

President, Global Women Speakers
Email: speak@GlobalWomenSpeakers.com
IG: @tinadlewis | FB: @tinadlewis| YouTube: @tinadlewis Linkedin: @tinadlewis | GlobalWomenSpeakers.com

AFFIRMATION

You see, in my humble opinion, Joy is not tangible. It's like the air. It's always there during every situation. The objective is to find it. Not once a week, twice a month, or every year but you can have pure Joy, 365 days a year. It's all about perspective and it's all up to you.

Dianne Lindsay

My name is Dianne Lindsay. I am a freshly new author of a book called *Godly Riddims* and The *Children's Heritage*. However, my Facebook name is Lemise Lar/ Dianne Lindsay.

AFFIRMATION

"I CAN DO ALL THINGS THROUGH CHRIST WHO STRENGTHENS ME."

Rev. Dr. Spencer C. Lofton Sr.

Rev. Dr. Spencer C. Lofton Sr. Retired United States Air Force Non-Commissioned Officer. Devoted husband to Lisa, diligent father of four, and loving grandfather of four (grandson) Jeremiah-pictured) Former AFJROTC Instructor, Successful Grant Writer, Coordinator of the White Springs Free SYEP and after-school programs for at-risk youths, Former United Way Board member, Former Mayor of White Springs, Florida, Professor at Heart Bible International University, Radio Personality of the hit Sunday morning radio show, "Meeting Every Need" (MEN). | My site (wjln887fm.wixsite.com). Member of Christ Central Church in Lake City, Florida under the leadership of Pastor Lonnie Johns.

AFFIRMATION

2 TIMOTHY 1:7 KJV "For God hath not given us the spirit of fear; but of power, and love, and of a sound mind."
May God bless us today with the peace of at-rest water.

Kami Love

My name is Kamille Smith. I am in the 7th grade and I'm currently 12 years old. I live in North Carolina, and I am the youngest girl of 2 older siblings. I have 2 older brothers. My favorite hobbies outside of school are shopping, cooking, doing hair, and playing with my dogs Diamond and Chico.

AFFIRMATION

My grief is real.
I grieve because I love.
I will take as much time as I need to grieve this loss.
I affirm Joy during this process.

Tafadhali Ngwy Lubungo

Tafadhali Ngwy Lubungo , Congolese national living in Cape Town South Africa. After graduating with a BA degree specializing in Public Administration, Development Studies, and politics, my ability to communicate with optimism and smiles opens new opportunities for becoming a tourist guide as a means of earning an income bringing joy to others and myself.

AFFIRMATION

I am Tafadhali Ngwy Lubungo, a regular person who urges his contemporaries to be in control of their delight with a brilliant grin that becomes a symbol of optimism, inspiring the world to embrace happiness with one beautiful smile at a time.

Apostle Tamela Lucus

Apostle Tamela Lucus is the Pastor of *Come Home Stop Talking About It.* She published her first book in 2015 and was a part of her first anthology in 2019, and various magazines. Her first single is called When I was Nothing God loves me. She's married with adult children.

AFFIRMATION

I am healed from negativity.
I am free to choose life, love, and peace.
I am delivered from unforgiveness.
I am free to be creative.
I am so happy that God allowed me to be a light to all children.
I am a motivator. *Iron sharpens iron * Proverbs 27:17*

Dr. Khafilah Malik

Dr. Malik has over fifteen years as an educator serving students in the capacity of a classroom teacher and administrator. Dr. Malik's expertise and background in education have allowed her to work in international schools in Africa and public and charter schools in America. She is a mother of an autistic son, and she has traveled to over 33 countries of which 11 have been with her son. Dr. Malik continues to work and empower children with Learning Disabilities, especially children on the Autism Spectrum.

AFFIRMATION

"Suffer little children, and forbid them not, to come unto me: For such is the kingdom of heaven." — Matthew 19:14

Guia Marie Marcaida

I am Guia Marie C. Marcaida, twenty-two years old, and a graduate of the Bachelor of Secondary Education Major in English. I am working as a novelist on *Stary Writing*, a digital writing app. I'm not famous, but I love writing, and that's what matters.

AFFIRMATION

According to the book of *Psalm 31:24, "Be strong and take heart, all you who hope in the Lord."* Let's continue to put our hope in God, and He will bless us with the courage and joy that no one or nothing can give us aside from Him.

Jennifer Marcus

Jennifer Marcus is a highly sought-after youth and adult keynote speaker, empowerment and resiliency coach, tv producer, and successful business owner. Jennifer currently owns 9 businesses including 2 speaking businesses and a nonprofit. Jennifer has been challenged, and overcome, by issues related to racism, physical & emotional abuse, and abandonment.

AFFIRMATION

"I am a beacon of strength and resilience, inspiring others with my unwavering determination."

Dr. Angela Marshall

Faith in God and her journey in life, shaped her life for leadership, service, and a passion for nurturing and empowering all those who crossed her path. She believes the cornerstone of success in life starts with faith in God and a consistent prayer life.
Facebook: https://www.facebook.com/4angelamarshall
Instagram: 4dr.angelammarshall

AFFIRMATION

Trust in the Process
Proverbs 3:5-6
Trust in the Lord with all thine heart; and lean not unto thine own understanding. In all thy ways acknowledge him, and he shall direct thy paths.

____
____
____
____
____
____
____
____
____
____
____

Patricia Marston

My name is Patricia Marston, Bestselling Author of the book *My Extraordinary Son – Bradley.* I was born and raised on the beautiful island of Jamaica. I studied Management Studies in Jamaica, and Biology in the US I am the owner of BEYOND THE SUNSET LLC. NY. Writing the blogs on my website helped in my grief process. Visit my website at www.beyondthesunset.net

AFFIRMATION

I AM loved. I AM successful.
I AM aligned with my highest good.
I AM noticing new opportunities.
I AM taking steps every day to live a successful and purposeful life. I AM becoming better with every passing day.
I AM proud of the person that I am and will become.
I AM blessed and favored. I AM who God says I AM.

Melsades McIntosh-Martin

My name is Melsades McIntosh-Martin, a daughter, mother, and grandmother. I was born on the beautiful Island of Jamaica. I attended St. Jude's Primary School and Wolmers Girls High School. I have been employed for 13 years as a Radiation Oncology Nurse in Central Florida. I have been a nurse for 40 years. I love to travel, love to spend quality time with my family and I love retail therapy. (When the going gets tough, the tough goes shopping). I am a born-again Christian and a Deaconess in my church.

AFFIRMATION

I AM a leader and not a follower.
I AM the product of a strong black woman.
I AM thankful for the friends and family God has Blessed me with. I decree and declare that tomorrow will be better than yesterday. I AM important, heads turn when I enter a room.
I AM healing physically, emotionally, and spiritually.
I AM who God says I AM.

Dr. Tanya F. Mattox

Dr. Tanya F. Mattox is a Medical Business Professional
Owner: In Focus Coaching Services, LLC,
Speaker: WEF Bangalore, India on Domestic Violence Awareness
EOTO org. Social Etiquette.
Author:
Young Adult 101
Contributor: " The Divine Feminine-My Relationship with God."

AFFIRMATION

I am Worthy.
I am Loved.
I am Intelligent.
I am Compassionate.
I am Powerful.

Diane Maupin

Diane Maupin is a Dallas native with a deep-rooted connection to both the community & businesses. Living through devastation and grief allows Diane to mentor and inspire others through her speaking and coaching business. Diane is co-owner of 2 other businesses and is working on 2 books and an education program.

AFFIRMATION

I acknowledge my grief and permit myself to heal at my own pace.

Melody McDaniels

Melody McDaniels is an Author, Entrepreneur, Certified Mental Health First Aider, CEO, and founder of DEDICATED TO SAVING LIVES INC. (a non-profit organization), Philanthropist, etc. Visit dedicatedtosavinglives.org to learn more about her and the organization.

AFFIRMATION

Nurture your soul through meaningful connections, weaving threads of joy into your relationships.

Michelle McKenney

Michelle McKenney was born in Brooklyn New York and currently resides in Raeford North Carolina. Mrs. McKenney is married to Samuel and has two dogs. Michelle is a Veteran of the United States Army and is currently the Chief Executive Officer of Ugly Essentials a natural skin, hair, and beard care business.
John 5:5 | Isaiah 55:8-9
FB: @michelle McKenney
IG: @ mychelle2002
Email: michellemckenney1972@gmail.com
Website: www.michelleymckenney.com

AFFIRMATION

I am proud of how I talk to myself when I wake up in the morning.

Natalie McKinnie

Natalie McKinnie is the CEO of Natalie McKinnie Agency LLC and New Mantle Enterprises, LLC. She recently published her first book, *A New Crown of Glory: Finding Purpose in the Midst of Tragedy*. Connect with her on Facebook, LinkedIn, and at www.newmantlemediagroup.com for her latest publications.

AFFIRMATION

I am trusting in God's plan for my life. My tomorrow is in His hand. I will be prosperous according to His will and no harm will come to me. I have hope and a future governed by His love for me.

Adriane M. McLeod

Adriane M. McLeod is a published author, certified life coach and motivational speaker who is dedicated to inspiring and serving women. Adriane's message of hope, faith, and love is very empowering as she shares her testimony of heartache, loss, and survival. Visit www.adrianemmcleod.com for booking and information.

AFFIRMATION

I'm proud of you for choosing HEALING.
I'm proud of you for choosing to face your PAIN.
I'm proud of you for choosing FREEDOM.
Choosing to let go of the trauma and healing is not easy but YOU'RE CHOOSING YOU

Dr. Brenda Miller

Dr. Brenda Miller is an educator, accredited event designer, wedding planner, small business owner, realtor, and retired federal employee. She is the proud mom of one son and three beautiful grandchildren.
You can connect with her on Facebook.

AFFIRMATION

Find joy in the journey, relishing each step you take towards your aspirations.

Angela M. Mitchell

Angela M. Mitchell is an award-winning international best-selling author, international speaker, Certified Content Marketing Specialist, Digital Marketing Strategist, and more. She helps women entrepreneurs build boss brands using quality content that converts.
Connect with her on Facebook at https://www.facebook.com/angiethemarketer and https://www.back2her.org/

AFFIRMATION

"Joy is my birthright, and I choose to invite it into my life every day. I find joy in the present moment and allow it to fill my heart with gratitude and positivity. I am worthy of experiencing joy and will actively seek it out." Angela M Mitchell

____

____

____

____

____

____

____

____

____

____

Dr. H. T. Mohair

Dr. H.T. Mohair embodies a versatile life as a gospel minister, engineer, and successful business magnate. Alongside Dr. Jacqueline Mohair, they nurture a family of four children and revel in the blessings of seven beloved grandchildren.

AFFIRMATION

Embrace the divine tapestry of joy woven into your life. Open your heart to God's blessings, finding joy in every step of your journey. Trust in His plan, and let gratitude illuminate the pathway, guiding you toward the profound joy embedded in the sacred blessings bestowed upon you.

Dr. Jacqueline Mohair

Ambassador Mohair, Bridging Gaps and Changing Lives, She is a nationally known Transformational Business and Life Strategist, Advocate, Professor, Life Coach, Minister, Serial Entrepreneur, and Ambassador to the UN. She is an author who has written inspirational books on empowerment and entrepreneurship, teaching Women from all walks of life how to win through faith. Dr. Mohair is a premiere Life Coach helping women to turn their passion into profits and dreams into reality. An advocate for change, who is passionate about empowering people to succeed in life and business, teaching mankind how to birth vision and turn their pain into purpose. Her motto is "You were created by a creator who's given you the Power to Create from the Well Within".

AFFIRMATION

I am the Righteousness of Christ! The Greater One lives in Me! I can do all things through Christ that strengthens me! I am more than a Conqueror! I am that I am! I can do exploits because they know their God is unstoppable.

Morgan Mohair

Morgan Mohair, a spirited 9th grader and cheerleader, aspires to become an anesthesiologist. With contagious enthusiasm on the cheer squad and a determined focus on her academic journey, Morgan embodies dedication and ambition in pursuing her dream career in medicine.

AFFIRMATION

I am a radiant force of positivity, spreading joy with each cheer. Surrounded by genuine friends, I embrace the magic of shared dreams and laughter. In the highs and lows, my spirit shines brighter. I am a cheerleader in life, and through friendship, I rediscover joy in every moment.

Myles Mohair

Myles Mohair, a determined 11th-grade football player, combines gridiron prowess with entrepreneurial dreams. With an eye on the future, he aspires to carve his path as a real estate mogul and insurance sales expert. Balancing athletic dedication with a hunger for success, Myles embodies ambition and versatility in pursuit of his aspirations.

AFFIRMATION

In life's tough game, I choose resilience over surrender, seeing challenges as opportunities. Every hardship is a chance to grow stronger. I embrace the struggle, learn from it, and find joy in my journey. I play with determination, praying for victories both on the field and in life.

Dr. Cheryl Monroe

Dr. Cheryl Monroe Served 28 years in the U.S. Army. She is the Founder and CEO of CK Management and Consultant Group, The Cleaning Advantage, and co-founder of a nonprofit whose mission is to empower and educate women. Cheryl is a native of Atlanta, GA. She is married to Ken; they have two sons and two grandchildren.

AFFIRMATION

Encouraging words, acts of kindness, and genuine smiles contribute to the contagious nature of joy. It is a powerful practice that creates a profound effect in our communities. May our lives be filled with exhilarating joy that inspires all to find their happiness.

Jabarrie Monsano

Jabarrie Monsano, a rising literary force, achieved bestseller status with *Image In The Mirror III*, marking his second literary triumph. A diligent student at LSU, he's set to graduate in 2024 with a Finance degree. Jabarrie seamlessly blends academia and artistry, leaving an indelible mark on both fronts.
Website: www.jabarriemonsano.com

AFFIRMATION

In moments of quiet reflection, seek the source of true joy. It's not found in fleeting pleasures or worldly acclaim but in embracing gratitude and faith. Let joy be your compass, guiding you toward a heart full of love, purpose, and divine contentment.

Nadia Monsano

Nadia Monsano is a 6X international bestselling author, marketing and branding specialist and a retired veteran staff sergeant after serving 10 years in the US Army. While in the military Nadia served one tour in Iraq and earned the Iraqi Freedom Medal of Honor. Nadia started her own company My Sister Keeper in February 2020. My Sister Keeper is a branding and marketing agency that offers graphic design. Nadia has worked with women all over the United States and Internationally to help them launch their businesses and show up in the digital market professionally.

AFFIRMATION

I abide in the love of the Father and keep His commandments therefore my love is full. I rejoice in hope as I am patient in trials while being constant in prayer. I will remain in the presence of the Lord for in His presence is the fullness of joy.

KJ Montgomery

KJ Montgomery is a 4x best-selling author, fibromyalgia advocate, jewelry designer, and photographer.
She's featured in several publications, is a contributing writer, and was on a billboard in Times Square (NYC).
She has a Bachelor's degree. Her goal is to bring awareness about the painful condition and to support those who have fibromyalgia.

AFFIRMATION

Rest assured that God will empower you to achieve whatever seems impossible. Never give up on anything. You are strong. Keep the faith and remember that God is by your side. You're never alone as you travel through life. Remain positive, peaceful, and joyful! Live your life to the fullest!!

LeTysha N. Montgomery

LeTysha Montgomery is a best-selling award-winning author, empowerment speaker, podcast host (Endometriosis: Journey to Butterfly), endometriosis advocate & jewelry designer (Stand Out Style). LeTysha won the Certificate of Achievement Global Impact Award & speaks about advocating for your health.
Connect with LeTysha on Facebook at Author LeTysha Montgomery & https://author-letysha.square.site.

AFFIRMATION

In life, don't be afraid to take the next step or move to the next level. Never allow yourself to become stagnant because of fear. If there is something that you want, do it now. Some things are only once-in-a-lifetime opportunities!

____

____

____

____

____

____

____

____

____

____

Mary Moore

Mary Moore intro I am a flawed woman of God who through many life traumas and challenges I realize. I have a great purpose. As a single mother entrepreneur who as a child and young adult, my deepest and constant prayer was for me to not wake up the next morning. But I pressed! I'm here! I've realized that there is a great calling on my life. My trauma had to be part of my journey to help uplift or guide anyone I can through their emotional journey to emotional healing.

Mary Louise
http://www.youtube/letstalkaboutit
Instagram @ mary_louise_lets_talk_about_it

AFFIRMATION

You are who God says you are. The head and not the tail. God makes no mistakes in His creations. Press towards another day, God has great promise and purpose for your life. You will reap your harvest if you faint not.

____

____

____

____

____

____

____

Yonelle Moore Lee, Esq.

The Honorable Yonelle Moore Lee, Esq. is an attorney, mediator, business owner, and elected official. She is a wife, mother, and woman of God. Yonelle is a breast cancer survivor who overcomes every obstacle in her path. She is authentic, gives more than she receives, and loves serving her community.

AFFIRMATION

Today, I choose JOY. Despite my situation or circumstances.
I choose JOY and to always be my most fearless, authentic, and truest self. I choose JOY and trust that I will overcome any obstacles. I choose JOY and know that I am always worthy.

Latasha Morgan, M.Div, MA

Latasha S. Morgan is a Certified Life Coach and Board-Certified Master Christian Mental Health Coach. She is the owner of Majestic Talks, LLC, and host of *The Majestic Talks Show*, where she offers purpose coaching.
Connect with her on Facebook, Majestic Talks LLC, The Majestic Talks Show, and at www.majestictalks.com.

AFFIRMATION

I am God's masterpiece and He created me to do good works because He loves me. Regardless of what I feel, see, experience, or hear, I know that God has imparted something to me that has the power to effect change in the lives of people.

Kyshone Moss

Kyshone Moss is a wife, mother, nurse and child of GOD. Born in Hammond, Indiana.
Connect with her at kyshonemoss@gmail.com

AFFIRMATION

Radiate kindness and compassion, channeling their transformative power into your joy-filled existence.

Michelynn Moss

Michelynn Moss is a 5X Bestselling International Author. She has penned books in the genres of Inspiration, Domestic Violence Mental illness, and Poetry. With an innate talent for storytelling and a passion for shedding light on important topics, her books have touched the lives of countless individuals, offering hope, empowerment, and profound insights into the human condition.
https://www.facebook.com/michelynn.moss
https://instagram.com/michelynnmoss

AFFIRMATION

"Don't compromise yourself. You are all you've got." ~ Betty Ford
"Those who bring sunshine to the lives of others cannot keep it from themselves." ~ James Barrie
"After the verb 'to Love', 'to Help' is the most beautiful verb in the world." ~ Bertha Von Suttner

____
____
____
____
____
____
____
____

Dr. Petrice M. McKey-Reese

Dr. Petrice M. McKey-Reese is a retired veteran, published author, certified coach, wife, mother, grandmother, and Child of God. She loves to help people.

Connect with her on Facebook at Dr-Petrice McKey-Reese The Author, on Instagram under her name, her website is https://www.authorpetricemckeyreese.com/, email is mckeyreesepm@yahoo.com and her cell is 918-770-3654.

AFFIRMATION

I am a Child of God.
I am too blessed to be stressed.
I am proud of all God has allowed me to accomplish.
I am loved.
I am responsible for my happiness. My opinion of me is more important to me than anyone else's opinion of me.

____

____

____

____

____

____

____

____

Venecia Monsano Thomas

Venecia Monsano Thomas, hailing from Trinidad's enchanting shores, embarked on her literary journey as a first-time author. Married for three decades, she cherishes the joys of motherhood and grand motherhood. Her debut captures the essence of her rich experiences and the vibrant tapestry of island life.

AFFIRMATION

I am filled with joy and gratitude for all the wonderful blessings in my life, and I choose to focus on the positive and joyful moments that surround me. Every day, I allow joy to fill my heart and guide me toward happiness and fulfillment in all aspects of my life.

Barbara Morrison-Williams

Rev. Barbara hails from London, England. She is an ordained minister and an award-winning educator. She has been married to Bishop Gerald C. Williams for 27 years and they have an adult daughter, Natalee Simone. Rev. Barbara is currently building her educational consulting business.
https://www.facebook.com/barbara.morrisonwilliams/
https://www.linkedin.com/in/barbaramwilliams/
https://www.instagram.com/barbaramwilliams/

AFFIRMATION

Joy is a gift, so I choose to walk in it daily.

Dr. Barbara Neely

Dr. Barbara Neely is the CEO of Mamas Brown Sugar and a Board-Certified Esthetician. She is a two-time Best-Selling author of the books, *Finding Joy in The Journey* and *Joy Comes in The Morning*. Dr. Barbara is an Ambassador for *Black Family Magazine* and has a show on *Rethink Network* titled, *Reignite with Dr. Barb.* Barbara is passionate about helping other women rise from the ashes of life and helping them discover their God-given talents.

AFFIRMATION

Today is a gift, and I embrace it with positivity.
I begin each day with a grateful heart.
I'm happy and grateful for having loving people in my life.
I am worthy and deserving of my beautiful dreams.
I greet each day with gratitude, hope, and positivity.

Evelyn Nelson

Evelyn Nelson- There have been some silver flashes of devastation along with Blessings in my life. Been singing since 1964 in a foster home. Between the murder of my biological mother whom I never knew and my dad's murder during our loving relationship. My healed heart causes me to sing forgiveness and love.
Silver Streak Lady: Listen to Silver Streak Lady by Evelyn Nelson 7 on #SoundCloud https://on.soundcloud.com/BJCRV
The Loved Fugitive https://youtu.be/kvQDZHAqbTw

AFFIRMATION

No matter the good or ugly past in our lives that we see, we can count it all joy, joy unspeakable and full of glory. It's to bring God glory after all in Him we live, move, and have our being. So why not exhale the pain and inhale true bliss?

____

____

____

____

____

____

____

____

____

Shari Nichelle

Shari Nichelle is from the state of Maryland, a proud mother, military Veteran, educator, published author, actor, model, voiceover artist, and a Baltimore Ravens fan!
Connect with her on Instagram @iam_sharinichelle or by email at sharinichelle@gmail.com.

AFFIRMATION

I acknowledge my need to control the things in my life and I choose to let them go. I actively give God the honor as the head of my life and in effect, I have found everlasting joy!

Dr. Thomasina D. Nicholas

Dr. Thomasina is the wife of William, mother, grandmother, ordained minister, retired 20 Yr. Army Veteran and social worker. She earned a B.S. in Christian Counseling /Mental Health, an M.A. in Theology /Christian Education, and a D.Min. She is a member of AACC, NAACP, CASA, and ADO Military Sorority.

AFFIRMATION

1). I will never forget the blessings that are bestowed upon me, nor take them for granted.
2). Forgive others, God forgave me.
3). Work on myself and as I work on me God is healing my hurts.
4). Bring Everything Near and Everything Far under Subjection. Submit to God.

Tasha Nicole

Tasha Nicole, a resilient Aquarius and devoted mother, embodies strength and determination. A true go-getter, she navigates life's challenges with grace, driven by a deep commitment to her family. Tasha's spirit shines through her unwavering dedication and the love she pours into every aspect of her life.

AFFIRMATION

I am Tasha Nicole—Aquarius, mother, and a beacon of strength. I embrace joy's restoration with resilience. My spirit, unwavering, illuminates life's tapestry with laughter, love, and enduring joy. In every challenge, I find opportunities for renewal. I am the architect of my happiness, creating a masterpiece of joy and strength.

Shywanna Nock

Shywanna Nock is a mother of three. A motivational speaker and author of *Cancer had my body, but it didn't have my mind*. Co-author of *Joy Comes in the Morning* and *My sister helped me heal*. Founder of Nay-Nay's Inspirations, CEO of Marketing Financial and Creative Services of Onpointradio Station, and Certified Life Coach. She loves giving encouraging words to uplift someone's day. You can connect with her at www.shywannanock.com or empoweryourself76@gmail.com.

AFFIRMATION

I am able. I am better
I am covered. I am whole
I am restored. I am healed
I am saved by his grace
I am covered by the blood
I am more than a conqueror

____

____

____

____

____

____

____

____

Cinderella Ochu

Cinderella Ochu is a PhD candidate at the University of Johannesburg, South Africa. She is a wife, mother, medical historian, and author. She enjoys spending time with her family.

Facebook- Cinderella Amos
https://www.facebook.com/cinderella.amos?mibextid=ZbWKwL
Twitter- @cinderellaamos
Instagram- @cindyochu
LinkedIn- Cinderella Ochu
Blog- Cindy Amos
Facebook Fan Page

AFFIRMATION

I am chosen. I am blessed. I am enough!

Candace Okin

Three-time published author and writer, Candace Okin uses the written word to inspire, educate, entertain, and assist others. She enjoys engaging with the community around books, literacy, philanthropy, and authorship. She holds a Bachelor's in Journalism from Texas Southern University and a Master's in Psychology from Houston Baptist University.
For more information, visit candaceokin.com.

AFFIRMATION

I was born with a purpose. I was destined for great things. I am here to make a positive difference. I will fulfill my God-assigned purpose. I am a creative being. I am purposeful and intentional in my purpose. I am gifted and infinitely loved. I am God's perfect creation.

Adeola Oladele

Adeola Oladele is an IT Analyst, her passion for young girls is evidenced in her podcast and monthly meeting tagged *EZ Breezy Girls Night*. She is also a wedding planner, serial entrepreneur, content creator, podcast host, young woman advocate and soon-to-be-published author.

AFFIRMATION

You are beautiful, you are bold, you are unique, you are special. You are not a mistake, and you have a purpose. You were put on earth to touch at least one life. You are confident, you are a value-adding agent, and you are self-sufficient and balanced.

Issata Oluwadare

Issata Oluwadare is a dynamic leader with ten years of leadership experience in the private and non-profit sectors. She is also a content creator, three-time #1 bestselling author, entrepreneur, motivational speaker, certified life coach, consultant for women in leadership & business, and founder of The EZ Breezy Life.
Learn more at www.ezbreezy.life and www.issatao.com.

AFFIRMATION

"Go and enjoy the choice of food and sweet drinks and send some to those who have nothing prepared. This day is holy to our Lord. Do not grieve, for the joy of the LORD is your strength." - Nehemiah 8:10

Arletha Orr

Arletha Orr is an American author from Mississippi. It was when her world collapsed that she discovered her true calling in life. With her enthusiasm, she hopes to selflessly serve others and show them that there is life after death. Orr is an Author, Publisher, and Certified Grief Coach.
www.iShallLive.com

AFFIRMATION

I am fearfully and wonderfully made!
I can have whatever God says I can have.
Just because it hadn't happened, does not mean God has forgotten about me. I stand on the word and promises of God.
I can and I will accomplish everything I want in life.

Sharone Pack

Theressa "Sharone" Pack is the Founder and Executive Director of Storge's (Stor-gay) House. Her nonprofit is dedicated to empowering single mothers through mental health awareness, financial literacy, educational support, and goal setting. With a Business Administration degree and as a Certified Life Coach, she is committed to helping them on their journey to success and well-being.

AFFIRMATION

Each day harnesses the power of discipline to shape a brighter future. Do this with unwavering focus, faith, and self-control. Keep your dreams alive, press forward, and know that with perseverance, you will find the keys to success and fulfillment. Trust in your abilities, for you are stronger than you think.

Jeremy O. Peagler

Jeremy O. Peagler is an ordained minister and public speaker with over 20 years of ministry experience. He has served in a multitude of ministry positions throughout the United States and abroad. Jeremy is a 23-year Veteran of the United States Air Force and has a bachelor's degree in business administration.

AFFIRMATION

Life is but a vapor. Therefore, I am committed to maximizing every gift God has given me to make the greatest impact in the earth.

Tikita Peagler

Tikita Peagler is the author of Undisturbed and Well Done. She is a credentialed Christian Life Coach, blogger, and public speaker. She has a bachelor's degree in Technical Management and is a US Air Force Veteran. Tikita lives in San Antonio, Texas with her husband and three children. See www.tikitapeagler.com.

AFFIRMATION

Life is but a vapor; therefore, I am determined to live well. I am loved by God and committed to His cause. I choose light over darkness, hope over despair, and kindness over cruelty.

Monique Pearson

Monique Pearson is the CEO of Soaring W/O Limits Enterprises, founder of Professionista a charity organization, and more. Connect with her on Facebook, Instagram, and at www.soaringwolimits.com

AFFIRMATION

My success is unlike anyone else's, and the more I share it with others, the more successful I become.

T.K. Peoples

TK Peoples is a teacher-librarian. At a young age, she knew she would be a writer. While working as a school librarian, T.K. saw the need for more bilingual books for children, which sparked her writing career. She believes that faith in God is the key to success. She has become a best-selling author of several children's and adult books.
Website: www.anortbooks.com
All Social Media Platforms: @anortbooks

AFFIRMATION

Today, I release the desire for revenge. I choose to forgive and trust in God's perfect justice. My heart is a sanctuary of peace, free from resentment. I embrace divine wisdom, leaving room for God's repayment. In forgiveness, I find strength, and in mercy, I discover true liberation.

Jada Perteet

Jada Perteet, a skilled cosmetologist and dedicated educator, balances her professional prowess with motherhood to Kingston Perteet. Her passion for beauty intersects with her commitment to education, embodying a nurturing spirit both in her career and family life.

AFFIRMATION

Embrace the present moment with mindful awareness, finding joy in each breath. In stillness, I discover the beauty of now, cultivating gratitude for the simple miracles that surround me. Today, I choose mindfulness, weaving tranquility into the fabric of my existence for a life of joyful living.

Rev. Unnia L. Pettus, Ph.D.

Reverend Unnia L. Pettus, Ph.D., is the Founder of Nobody But God Ministries and Pettus PR. She is a 4-time cancer, stroke, and domestic violence survivor, author, and advocate. You can follow her on social media at @DrUnniaPettus, and connect with her at www.UnniaPettus.com

AFFIRMATION

Without faith, it is impossible to please God.

Sharita Phillip

Pastor Sharita is the Senior Pastor of Allow God Deliverance Outreach Ministries, International, a published author, and the Founder of Proverbs 31 Women Ministry (2012) and Ladies of Grace Ministry (2018). She is a wife of 24 years and a mother of three amazing children.

AFFIRMATION

Father, I trust you with my life and every circumstance I may face; help me count it all joy and lean not to my understanding when the trials of life seem to be caving in on me. Today, I choose to rejoice in every circumstance I may face, good or bad, because you promised never to leave or forsake me; therefore, I take Joy in knowing that you are with me. In Jesus' name, Amen.

Constance Phillips

Constance Gray was born and raised in Saint Louis, Mo. She has 3 beautiful children who are her inspiration. Constance is a 2x Amazon Best Selling Author. She is a co-author in *Pendulum of a Mother's Love and Finding Joy in the Journey*. She is an entrepreneur by trade running a family-owned janitorial and logistics business. Constance is enjoying being on a new walk of faith with God. She enjoys attending worship services and spending time with family.

AFFIRMATION

There's nothing I can't do without Jesus. He places a new batch of joy in my heart daily. I embrace joy and gently release anything that is not joy! I will decree and declare that joy will follow me all the days of my life.

Sheair Phillips

SheAir Phillips is a therapist, photographer, and more. She works in the community as an Infant Family Specialist providing strategies for early intervention for infants and their caregivers to strengthen their attachment and development of relationships.
The inspirational gift of capturing moments in time for her clients in addition to her daughter being her muse motivated her to develop a photography business in 2020.
Connect with her on Facebook, Tovya Renee or Skai Photography, and Instagram, @Skaiphotographyy.

AFFIRMATION

I am released from the past. I am not broken.

Julia Pierre

Evangelist Julia Pierre is a mother, grandmother, insurance agent, and business owner. Fulfilling 26 years of ministry in many capacities. Internationally, compelled to birth and encourage many to embrace spiritual purpose that enables their natural existence. Ordained by the Apostolic anointing of Bishop James and Pastor Lisa Keys of Pennsylvania.

AFFIRMATION

As a reflection of illuminating responsibility and integrity to myself and others. I will be true and accountable to biblical values and principles. I believe through Jesus Christ you have no limits to what you can achieve. **I Give Myself Permission to Shine!**

Davonte Pinkney

Davonte, an enthusiastic individual with a deep love for driving, is on a journey to explore new horizons. While he hasn't yet experienced the workplace, his passion for the open road reflects his determination and desire to embark on a fulfilling career path. Excited to embrace new opportunities.

AFFIRMATION

"I am a capable and resilient individual. I trust in my abilities and remain open to new opportunities. With determination and positivity, I will attract the perfect job that aligns with my skills and passions. I am one step closer to finding the employment I desire."

Dr. Bernadette Plummer

Bernadette is a proud mother, Aunt, and US Army veteran. Her passion is serving her community whether it is locally or internationally. She enjoys her family, traveling, cooking, reading, and meeting new people. She is also a member of Zeta Phi Beta Sorority Incorporated.

AFFIRMATION

Wake up each morning to be intentionally infectious with positivity.

Felicia Pouncil

As a former educator turned retirement planning and insurance agent, I leverage my passion for teaching to empower individuals with financial literacy. I'm a devoted mother dedicated to securing financial futures. My mission is to educate and protect one family at a time.
www.lsfg.info

AFFIRMATION

Always remember the powerful words of *Philippians 4:13: 'I can do all things through Christ who strengthens me.'* In times of pain and struggle, let this verse be your guiding light, reminding you of the limitless strength that resides within you through faith.

Kaidynce Pugh

Kaidynce Pugh is a high school-bound freshman, and daughter of co-author Dr. Radiance Rose. She dominates in basketball while inspiring her teammates to greatness. Beyond her sporting prowess, Kaidynce is also embarking on a literary adventure, co-authoring in Joy 365, showcasing her multifaceted talents.

AFFIRMATION

I personify unwavering resilience as I navigate my courageous journey, with hope as my guiding light. In the face of challenges, I rise with strength and determination, knowing that I can overcome any hurdle that comes my way.

Patrick Purcell

Dr. Patrick Purcell is a Fayetteville, NC native. He is a prolific visionary and preacher. Dr. Purcell is the Founder of Kingdom Alliance Global Ministries and "God Conversations. "He endeavors to empower and equip God's people. His philosophy is "*I Live to Love you and Fight for you Daily*!"
www.facebook.com/godconversations
God-Conversations - YouTube

AFFIRMATION

Today, I decree that I am focused, not distracted. I choose to live in stability. I am not unbalanced. I will not retreat but face every season with the revelation of God. My seek shall confirm my faith's assignment and God will make success tangible according to my seek.

____

____

____

____

____

____

____

____

____

____

Dr. Tiffany Quinn

Dr. Tiffany Quinn is a social worker, certified life coach, and the founder of T.J Quinn Ministries LLC. With over 30 years of experience serving in her community, she has developed a wealth of expertise in trauma-informed mental health working with individuals with emotional and behavioral disorders.

AFFIRMATION

I find joy in the small moments of life - the warmth of the sun, the sound of birds, and the love of those around me. I am grateful for every smile, and I face challenges with strength and resilience. I choose to focus on the positive and embrace the joy and delight that life brings.

Demowah Quoiyan

Demowah Quoiyan is a passionate servant of the highest King, Jesus, who believes in the word of God and the power of prayer. She is a Mother, Wife, Ambassador, Intercessor, Music Minister, Soldier, and, most importantly, a servant-leader. Her life shows how God can make everything beautiful in his time.

AFFIRMATION

Everyone deserves joy in their life. We must choose happiness in every moment of our lives. When we experience joy in our lives, we uplift others. Joy helps us push aside those negative feelings and emotions that affect our mood. It allows us to manage frustrations, disappointment and reduces stress.

Dr. Catovia Rayner

Dr. Catovia (Dr. Cat) , DHA, MPH, MSW, LCSW, is a cultural anthropologist, sociologist, social worker, and historian. As a professional speaker, she brings awareness to social and cultural issues related to underrepresented individuals and groups. The works she has created focus on bringing awareness to the Black Indigenous, People of Color (BIPOC) perspective in American culture. She is a certified Diversity and Inclusion Specialist with vast experience as a professional speaker. She can be found on Facebook @DrCatC
Website: www.urbanbutterfly.media
Email:drcat@urbanbutterflymedia.com

AFFIRMATION

I will succeed, I am loved, I know my worth.
I celebrate who I am in the spirit of GOD's Love.
I will take a moment to restore myself. I will seek help when needed.

Coach Gloria Raynor

Coach Gloria Raynor is a certified coach, inspirational speaker, spiritual counselor, and teacher. Author three published books, a best-selling author with *Barron with Purpose: Fertility in Dry Places.* Christmas inspiration and co-author of *Christmas with hot apple cider.* She shows individuals how to regain emotional health with spiritual wellness towards a balanced lifestyle.

AFFIRMATION

I affirm my power through Christ the source. My wisdom and knowledge to pursue my destiny through the guidance of the Holy Spirit. I was born to explore, replenish, and dominate earth with the word empowering others to live a full life sharing, caring, and loving in God's abundance.

Choose Joy

Dr. Latasha Ramsey-Cyprian

Dr. Latasha Ramsey- Cyprian a native of Louisiana is the owner of Optimum Life Credit Solutions. She is an Author, Speaker, Credit Repair Specialist, and Life Coach. Latasha aims to empower and inspire through financial literacy and challenges individuals to have a growth mindset.

Connect with Latasha at: info@optimumlifecreditsolutions.com

AFFIRMATION

Feed your spirit with uplifting thoughts, fueling a continuous wellspring of joy.

____

____

____

____

____

____

____

____

____

____

____

____

____

Pastor Beverly J. Renford

Pastor Beverly J. Renford is the Senior Pastor of The Greater Bethlehem Temple Pentecostal Church, Inc., is an international best-selling author, and an entrepreneur who teaches, encourages, mentors, and facilitates throughout the kingdom of God and literary advancements. She encourages and intercedes for God's people through the power of the Holy Ghost. Beverly is a contributing author in three published works: The wife to Elder Mark A. Renford, Mother of 8, and G-Maw to 7. Email:authorpastorbeverlyrenford@gmail.com

AFFIRMATION

"You are the whole package, unwrap yourself and blossom"

Alicia Rengel

I am Alicia Rengel from Miami, happily married with a loving son who is a doctor. I cherish my stepchildren, whom I affectionately call Love, Peace, and Joy, and adore my two granddaughters. For the past 42 years, I have been assisting immigrants with the support of a great lawyer.

AFFIRMATION

I embrace the Joy of the Lord and choose to grow where I am planted, finding constant joy in my relationship with God. My life flourishes as I trust in His divine plan, and I share this message of joy with others to inspire and encourage them.

Charlissa Rice

Charlissa Rice was born in Durham, NC. Graduated from the Illustrious North Carolina Central University in 2010 with a B.A. in Sociology. She is a wife, mother, and sister, and loves everything about fashion. Frugal Fab Fashion was founded in 2014, where she broadcast frugal fashion ideas, tips, and inspiration. She is an active member and Secretary of the Carolina Black Caucus at the University of North Carolina at Chapel Hill. A member of Swing Phi Swing, Social Fellowship Incorporated She is also a proud delegate of the Employee Forum at the University of North Carolina at Chapel Hill. She serves as the faculty advisor for Voices of Praise. She loves giving back to her community and inspiring others to do the same.

AFFIRMATION

You are loved just for being who you are, love and to be loved to exist no matter where you are.

Harriet Rice

Harriett Rice I was born in New Haven, Connecticut. I had one sibling, and he was a Psychoanalyst in Boston. I am a graduate of Sarah Lawrence College. I received a master's degree (MSW) from Columbia School of Social Work. I went on to receive a Certificate in Psychoanalytic Psychotherapy. I was married to the late Dr. Emmanuel Rice, Psychiatrist and Author of (Freud and Moses, The Long Journey Home).

Email: riceharr@icloud.com

AFFIRMATION

Open your heart to laughter, a powerful elixir for restoring joy.

Barry Stephens Ricoma

Barry S. Ricoma is a native of Brooklyn, New York, a Father to one son (Ryan), a 21-year Veteran of the Military Armed Forces (U.S. Army), and a Best Selling author.
Connect with him on Facebook, Barry.S.Ricoma, and at twowheeledfreedom.com.

AFFIRMATION

Let go of past burdens, making room for the vibrant joy of the present.

Evg. Dr. Debra Riddlespriger

Evg. Dr. Debra Riddlespriger is a best-selling author, soul coach, business coach, and songstress. She is empowered to minister the Love of God through evangelism and as a true worshipper. Her passion in ministry is to reach, teach, preach pray, and watch God work!

AFFIRMATION

Father, please continue to remind us that we always have the blessed opportunity to choose You in all circumstances. When choosing You, we choose peace, victory, and Joy. Thank You for Your unspeakable Joy! In Jesus' name, Amen.

Dr. Sophronia Winn Riley

Loves facilitating leadership through the lens of God's Word. A federal government worker with over 30 years of leadership experience. Developed a servant leadership program called *S*erving *O*thers by *L*eading, *E*ncouraging them to *S*erve (S.O.L.E.S.) for children and adults to understand how to serve God and as a leader. Solesconsult@gmail.com

AFFIRMATION

You have the authority over your life to decide how you would start your day. I decided that I want God to look at me every day and know through my character and conduct, that God is proud to call me His child and I am excited to know He is my Father.

Dr. Tina Riley

Team Lead and Security Programs Manager for the Department of Defense, Pentagon. Tina is a proud, retired, Air Force Veteran. She has earned an Applied Science, Bachelor of Science, and Master of Science degrees including an Honorary Doctorate from Cornerstone Christian University. Tina is also an independent Avon Consultant.

AFFIRMATION

The Truth of the Matter…Jesus is my Joy 365

Michele Roach

Poet. Author of the book, *Simply Love*, Executive Manager of *The Reverend and The DJ* Gospel Show, All Nations Radio Partnership Director, Past Marketing Director, Toastmasters International

AFFIRMATION

"Be cheerful no matter what; pray all the time; thank God no matter what happens. This is the way God wants you who belong to Christ Jesus to live." -1 Thessalonians 5:16-18
MSG

Jaden Robinson

Hi, my name is Jaden Robinson. I am a South Florida native, and current sophomore at Nova Southeastern University. I find joy in doing things that allow me to express my creativity.

AFFIRMATION

I choose to see the bright side in every situation.
I embrace joy even in challenging times.
I find joy in the small moments of life.

Dea. Kenneth Eric Robinson Sr.

Deacon Kenneth Eric Robinson Sr. is an educator, entrepreneur, co-author, and Executive Director of a nonprofit with 501C3. Email: kennethrobinson65@yahoo.com.

AFFIRMATION

EMPOWERING WISDOM WEALTH AFFIRMATION
I can overcome any money obstacles that stand in my way, I can achieve greatness and I am worthy of what I DESIRE.

Coach Vuyanzi Rodman

Coach Vuyanzi Rodman, a certified Life, Executive, and Career Coach with a Master's in Adult Education, sparks transformation. As host of *The Find Your Voice Show*, she empowers black women leaders. Globally influential, her purpose-driven journey nurtures transformative leaders. Her 2024 book release will empower women to heal, awaken, and transform.

AFFIRMATION

My divine joy springs from within me in all that I do, in who I love, and in what I possess. I embody unending joy.

Latrice D. Rogers

Latrice D. Rogers is a writer, mother of two young adults, an educator, and the author of *Evolution of Hummingbird*. After several challenging losses, she tapped into her faith and intentionally set out to make good memories.

Website: https://www.latricedrogers.com/
Facebook Group: Evolution of Hummingbird
IG: @ladaro | Twitter: @LaDaRo929

AFFIRMATION

I care for myself intentionally.
I am evolving and proud of who I'm becoming.
I am honest with myself and living authentically.
I strive to be the best version of myself every day.
I have everything I need because of God's plans for me.
I have JOY; my spirit is watered.

Dr. Patricia Rogers

"Unity In Service, Inc." is committed to creating speaking opportunities for business owners worldwide and takes pride in its efforts to support the global business community." Visibility Strategist, 2x Winning Intl. Public Speaker, 2x Intl. Best-Selling Author, Virtual Event Host & Organizer and Promoter.

AFFIRMATION

In the vibrant tapestry of social media, I am a unique thread, weaving connections and spreading positivity. My voice resonates, and my presence inspires. I embrace authenticity, radiating confidence and kindness. I amplify my true self, attracting a community that values and uplifts.
I shine brightly in this digital universe!

Nataylia Roni

Nataylia is a British Jamaican writer & artist.
Longlisted for the evening standards stories contest in London.
Also featured in PGE's anthology NYC.
Affiliated with The Robey Theatre Writers Lab and Mentor/Mentee.
Tenacious Spirit EP is available to download
+ One Woman Play
www.nataylia.com
@iamnataylia

AFFIRMATION

GOD'S CREATION IS

I AM

I AM BLESSED

I AM

Dr. Radiance Rose

Dr. Radiance L. Rose is professionally known as an award-winning, Certified Professional Life and Leadership Coach, Transformational Speaker, #1 Best-Selling Author, Entrepreneur, Professor, & SHE-EO/Founder of ViVi Cole Coaching & Consulting LLC. For 18 years, Dr. Rose has helped thousands of people transform their lives through coaching & mentorship.

AFFIRMATION

I am grateful for all my life's blessings and move through each day with grace and ease. I attract positivity and abundance, and I am thankful for every opportunity that comes my way. I focus on gratitude and grace, and my life is filled with unspeakable joy and peace.

Flavya Reeves Toefield

Flavya Reeves Toefield is a fearfully and wonderfully made woman who refuses to be bound by adversity. She is the Founder/ President of Duckie's Treasure Chest, Inc., wife of Jeremy Toefield, mother to Jonathan Paul Monnet, Jr., Jeremyiah & Lovely Toefield, and much more. Connect with her on Facebook (DuckiesTreasureChest) or via email (dtc2chron58@gmail.com).

AFFIRMATION

Jeremiah 29:11
For I know the plans I have for you, declares the Lord. Plans to prosper you and not harm you, and to give you hope for the future.
2 Corinthians 5:8
To be absent from the body, is to be present with the Lord.

____

____

____

____

____

____

____

____

____

____

Dr. Felicia Russell

"You can move from pain to purpose"
My intention is for you to know that we may struggle and face fears of the unknown, but you still can become who you were created to be through it all. You may encounter many defeats, but you will not be defeated. Sometimes we must go through the worst to get to the best.
Facebook: Felicia Russell

AFFIRMATION

Become Her
Become Him
You were chosen on purpose with a purpose.
The best thing you can do is believe you can.
I am happy about this version of me.
I love the woman that I am becoming, Unapologetically.
Things are happening for you and not just to you.

____

____

____

____

____

____

____

Dr. Alvina Ryan

Meet Dr. Alvina Ryan- best-selling author, change leader, passionate speaker, and life coach. She is the visionary author of books like *iPray On Purpose Because* and *iTestify On Purpose Because.*

Connect with Dr. Ryan:
https://www.alvinaryan.com
FB https://www.facebook.com/alvina.ryan
IG https://www.instagram.com/alvina__ryan/

AFFIRMATION

I affirm that this year is your year. You will live a life that will inspire and uplift everyone you meet. You will cultivate a spirit of ebullience while spreading love and boundless joy to everyone around you. With a genuine smile, you become a changemaker. This is my declaration.

____

____

____

____

____

____

____

____

____

____

Brenda Sawyer

Brenda is an Author and CEO who equips Christian Women between the ages of forty-five and sixty-five who have been abused with strategies to move from pain to purpose by encouraging, empowering, and transforming their lives through Biblical principles and teaching, while leaving an indelible legacy for posterity and confidence.

AFFIRMATION

I am in the right place at the right time, doing what God has called me to do for every right loving purpose according to His will. I will never give up because the joy of the Lord is my strength.

Amenna Scott

I have been sick with Systematic Lupus, Sexually Assaulted, Depressed, Suicidal Thoughts, and Experienced Death. Jesus brought me out and Now that I have been healed I want to walk into my calling as being a Spiritual Motivational Speaker to touch and turn other people towards God and doing my Father's business for the Kingdom.

AFFIRMATION

Trust in God doing trials and your struggles I know sometimes it's hard but that's when the trust comes in and I give Him all of you, your cares, and your worries.
Proverbs 3:5-6 Trust in the LORD with all thine heart; And lean not unto thine own understanding. In all thy ways acknowledge him, And he shall direct thy paths.

Dotty Scott

Dotty Scott, owner of Premium Websites, creates unique web designs, offering personalized solutions beyond "cookie-cutter" sites. Dotty, a best-selling author, and speaker, empowers small business owners to reach their goals.
Contact Dotty, who goes the extra mile at PremiumWebsites.net or AskDotty.com.

AFFIRMATION

Joy is a choice that I made today. I choose Joy!

Angela Sunday Cobb

My name is Angela Sunday Cobb. I'm the wife to Sous Chef Antron Cobb, and the mother to Aniyah, Isaiah, Adrianah, and Harmoney. I own a childcare center in Harker Heights, TX, We Play & More LLC. and I hold a master's degree in teaching. I love experimental cooking, traveling, and spending time with family.

AFFIRMATION

I thank God for everything that He has done in my life. I thank Him for always protecting me and my family. We are Blessed Beyond Measures.

Natasha Sunday Clarke, Hon. Ph.D.

Areas of mental health treatment, domestic violence, and diversity barriers. Dr. Natasha Sunday Clarke was born in Clanton, Alabama, however, she is a native of Winston-Salem, North Carolina. She is a certified Life Coach and Human Rights Consultant. In 1997 Dr. Clarke enlisted into the United States Army Reserves and upon graduating, in 2002, she received her commission into the Transportation Corps as a Second Lieutenant. Dr. Clarke was awarded the Presidential Lifetime Achievement award in 2023.

AFFIRMATION

Cherish those whom God has placed in your path, whether for a season or a reason.
Don't neglect your Spiritual, Physical, Emotional, Financial, or Mental Health.
Continue to Trust God in all things.
These affirmations allow me to focus on my Blessings each day.

Shari Sears

I served and retired from the Army. I am happily married and enjoy life to the fullest.

AFFIRMATION

I can, I will, and I believe.

Dr. Angela Seay

Dr. Angela Seay has never lost her drive or her New York state of mind. Educating others is a part of her DNA. Modeling her life after her Mantra, Healthy people are happy people and happy people show love. You can find me on social media @DrAngela Seay or D3HealthFitness

AFFIRMATION

Today is a great day to be intentional about spreading joy and making a positive impact on the lives of others. I am so grateful and happy that I have everything that I need for good health, a positive attitude, productivity, finance, balance, and continual growth.

Dr. Angela Sinkfield-Gray

Dr. Angela Sinkfield-Gray has over 40 years of experience in the field of advocacy, enrichment, and empowerment for women and children. She currently serves as the Executive Director of Daughters of Zion Global Initiatives, and The Supporting My Dream Project. She can be reached at daughtersofzionglobal.com

AFFIRMATION

God always causes me to triumph! 2 Cor. 2:14

Dr. Erica Sheffield

I am Dr. Erica Sheffield, the founder of Anchored 2 Teach, LLC and Dr. Erica Speaks. My journey of overcoming personal challenges fuels my passion for empowering others. As a mentor, international speaker, educator, and survivor of adversity, I inspire others to shed their masks and embrace their destinies. In essence, life's trials are steppingstones to atrium, Contact me at
www.drericaspeaks.com (website) info@drericaspeaks.com (email)
www.linkedin.com/in/drericasheffield
www.facebook.com/anchored2teach

AFFIRMATION

My strength is a source of radiant light. I am not defined by the scars of my past; but by my ability to bounce back. My unwavering commitment to helping others find their purpose is a testament to my character. I am a walking miracle!

____

____

____

____

____

____

____

____

____

Choyce Simmons

2x Amazon Best-Seller, co-author of *Joy 365*, releasing 2024. Founder of Beautiful Minds, LLC. Advocate, author, consultant, educational therapist, and certified grief support specialist, with a psychology degree and Double Master's in Human Service Counseling and Education, specializes in special education, grief & trauma interventions, empowering families, children, and communities for lasting impact. Connect:
www.choycesimmons.com
Simmonschoyce@gmail.com,beautifulmindsccllc@gmail.com
Facebook: ChoyceSimmons or BeautifulMindsLLC

AFFIRMATION

I am enough, just as I am; beautifully broken. In my healed wounds and mended cracks, I find strength, resilience, and a unique story that makes me who I am. I am a masterpiece, lovingly crafted with purpose. My worthiness is not defined by my past or the thoughts of others. I am constantly growing and improving, embracing my divine worth with grace and devotion each day.

____

____

____

____

____

____

Paulette Simmons

I am an MS Clinical Counselor & Certified Executive Coach, a Purpose Catalyst that helps people to recognize & discover their passions while allowing themselves to walk in their purpose so that they can live a more fulfilling life on purpose. I am also an author, international speaker, teacher, mentor, online course creator, and servant.

FB~@Living Life Strong | IG~@dearpaulie
LinkedIn~ Paulette Simmons
Email: simmonspn2019@gmail.com
Website: www.livinglifestrongcoaching.com

AFFIRMATION

"I choose to live a transparent life, where honesty and authenticity guide my every action. I trust that by being true to myself and others, I attract positivity and abundance into my life. I am grateful for the opportunity to live with integrity and inspire others to do the same."

Amber Sims

Amber Sims is a Sous Chef at Montclair State University, a business owner, an Army Vet, a mom to two and so much more. Connect with her on Facebook, Instagram, and website @ allthingsgoodcatering.com

AFFIRMATION

You are worthy and deserving of beautiful dreams, don't go through the storms alone.

Coach Teon Singletary

Multi-bestselling author, Speaker, Coach, and Neuroencoding Specialist, Coach Teon Singletary brings magnetic energy, inspiring you to live your best life with excellence. Visit this site to learn more: https://linktr.ee/TeonSingletary.

AFFIRMATION

The Power of Choice

We all have the power of choice. Depending on how we exercise that power will determine the outcome of our future. Live today to grow yourself and make better choices. It doesn't matter how big or small; each one counts. First, list the things you will choose to do differently. Next, all you must do now is execute those choices. If it's hard for you, pray and meditate on them daily. You have the power of choice. So, choose for today.

Demaryl Roberts-Singleton

Demaryl Roberts Singleton has a BS, MA, M.B.A., PgMP and is Best-Selling Author of *Her Story is My Story, Her Truth My Healing,* and *Finding Joy in The Journey Vol 2.* Demaryl retired in 2021 after serving 37 years of exceptional civilian service for the DoD. Demaryl has participated in countless community service activities. She is an active member of the National Council of Negro Women, Incorporated, Order of the Eastern Star, A.E.A.O.N.M.S. Misr Court #193, and The Links, Incorporated
Website https://demarylrobertssingleton.wordpress.com

AFFIRMATION

Proverbs 11:24-25
The world of the generous gets larger and larger; the world of the stingy gets smaller and smaller.
The one who blesses others is abundantly blessed; those who help others are helped.

____

____

____

____

____

____

____

Zariya Skai

Zariya Skai I am from the Metro Area of Michigan. I am a 6-year-old dancer, swimmer, and performer. I enjoy arts and crafts and always learn new things as I grow.

AFFIRMATION

Kindness is like magic; it makes hearts happy, and troubles disappear. You have the power to make someone's day brighter with your kind words and actions.

Spread smiles, share love, and be a superhero of kindness. Remember, you're amazing and your kindness matters. Keep shining, little star!

Darlene Smith

Darlene Smith is a chef, mother, grandmother, and an Amazon bestselling author, she enjoys reading, chess, tennis, and fashion. One of her other loves is traveling and learning new techniques. She believes in continually learning so that you can grow. She has spent over 20 years in the culinary industry. She can be reached at
darlene@oppiellc.com
IG: Chefdarlene602

AFFIRMATION

I can always find Joy in the promise of God's presence. I trust in Him and He let joy be restored in my life. During my darkest days.

Nakiea Smith

Nakiea Smith is from Alabama and currently resides in Georgia. Nakiea believes in learning something new every day. She is the founder and co-host of 21 Minutes or Less, a podcast that encourages self-care for entrepreneurs. She is also an author, and digital creator selling planners & journals on Amazon.

AFFIRMATION

God Given Gifts

My gifts are going to make room for me!
My gifts open doors for me!
My gifts are extraordinary!
I work on my gifts daily!
My gifts attract my tribe!
My gifts bring prosperity and abundance!
My gifts bring happiness and joy!
I am grateful!

Terrence Smith

Terrence Smith is a 15-year-old sophomore who loves his pet, Nuke. Terrence loves to swim, and learning to be a writer is an exciting new journey. Terrence dreams of being a mechanical engineer. Find more about Terrence and Nuke's Journey to adulthood on www.teennuke.com

AFFIRMATION

Embrace your faith, seek God's guidance, build positive relationships, discover your gifts, face challenges with joy, serve others, and stay connected with your faith community. Through this journey, you will find your purpose and a deeper connection with your Creator. God has great plans for you, and you are not alone in this walk of faith.

Dr. Theresa A. Smith

Dr. Theresa A. Smith has continually served this nation honorably since 1992. She presently serves as a Department of the Army Civilian in the Pentagon. She is a military spouse, former DOD Contractor, and U.S. Army Veteran. Dr. Smith was is an International Best-Selling Author and recipient of the President's Lifetime Volunteer Service Award.

AFFIRMATION

I am taking steps every day to live a successful and purposeful life. I live my dream every day, assisting and inspiring others to do the same.

Dalton Spence

Dalton Spence is a music teacher born, in Kingston, Jamaica. I attended St. George College in Jamaica, and I also attended The University of Technology (UTECH).
I am the second of three children. I spread light and love wherever I go, to empower people, especially the young and rejected. I am LOVE.

AFFIRMATION

I AM Successful. I AM Confident.
I AM Getting better and better every day.
I AM Grateful for abundant blessings.
I AM Strong.
I AM an inspiration to many.
I AM in perfect health.
I AM Having an exceptional day.
I AM Having a positive impact on the people I meet.
I AM who God says I AM.

Jaya Suganya Srinivasan

Jaya is a Homemaker. She serves on the Leadership Team at Church. Jaya is passionate about living as a witness for Christ in all areas of life. Through her online presence, Jaya spreads the fragrance of Christ on

Facebook: Jeya.s.srinivasan

Youtube. : Biblekeys4holylife

Instagram: biblekeys_4 holylife

AFFIRMATION

O Precious Child of God, lift your head...Walk in the Light. You are Worthy, Loved, and Cherished. Do not conform to the Pattern of this World but be Transformed. You are Here on earth with a Purpose and for a Purpose. Know your Identity in Christ!!!

Dr. Saundra E. Stancil

Dr. Saundra E. Stancil is an accomplished 40-year entrepreneur who has started eight successful businesses–all on a skinny budget while recovering from narcissistic abuse.
Gifted as a Teacher, Producer, and Leader, Dr. Stancil was born in our Nation's Capital over 40 years ago, and practices daily devotions. and coaches on business and personal success.
Her work has been featured on major television, print media, and the news.

AFFIRMATION

I AM Perfect for what God wants me to Do!
I AM a Child of God Who always remains connected to my Source: God uses me daily, hourly, and minute-by-minute.
I AM working diligently and my efforts Today CREATE Financial Freedom for Myself and for generations to come.

Gina Stockdall

Gina Stockdall has been working in graphic design and marketing since 2021. After partnering with organizations like Faith United Methodist Church and Richland Outreach Center, she has grown to offer marketing, design, and fundraising to nonprofits and churches.
Marilynjeannedesigns.com
facebook.com/marilynjeannedesigns
instagram.com/marilynjeannedesigns
linkedin.com/company/marilynjeannedesigns

AFFIRMATION

I know that all will be well today because I am held by my Heavenly Father who calls me His beloved.

Pastor Annette Sunday

Annette grew up in Birmingham, Alabama. Annette married Marcallus Sunday in 1978 and God blessed their marriage with five children.

Annette is Co-Pastor of Spiritual Macedonia Baptist Church in Saginaw, Michigan alongside her husband Pastor Marcallus Sunday.

Annette enjoys cooking, reading, sewing, shopping, helping others, and spending time with family.

AFFIRMATION

"I am so happy and grateful that God chose me and called me to be one of His Servants; a Minister."

"I am enjoying being a Minister."

"I am working towards a goal in ministry that is important to me, and that goal is to continue to encourage and lead people to Jesus Christ."

Pastor Marcallus Sunday

Pastor Marcallous Sunday was born in New York and raised in Alabama. However, he is a native of Winston-Salem, NC Pastor Marcallus Sunday is an Army Veteran Following his retirement, he transitioned his time to focus on his family and community. Pastor Sunday is married to Co-Pastor Annette Sunday

AFFIRMATION

I acknowledge my anxiety, but I choose to release it and let go of any negative thoughts or emotions. I trust that I am safe and capable of handling any situation that comes my way with the help of my Almighty God. I am strong, brave, and resilient.

Rosa Sylvester

Rosa Sylvester lives south of Atlanta, Georgia. She is a mother of three and is a fan of professional American football. Rosa enjoys journaling and spending time with God. She has made many discoveries in her journey with the Lord. Connect with her on Facebook and Instagram as "Rosa Sylvester".

AFFIRMATION

I look to the Lord for my joy and strength. I am His child, and he delights in me.

Karen Sztendel

I am Karen and together with my family we show you the land of Israel! Join us! I dedicate myself to a blog focused on the Spanish-speaking public. My name is Keren Noemi, I was born in Asunción Paraguay, since 2019 I began the adventure of creating content on social networks and sharing my life and trips throughout Israel.

AFFIRMATION

Shalom Haverim
If you can believe it, nothing is impossible! Don't be afraid, trust!
I wait for you so that together we can tour Israel, the land of the Bible!
Shalom Leculam, shalom for all!

Tyra Tate

Tyra Tate has served for 23 years as a school counselor and a Licensed Marriage and Family Therapist. She enthusiastically supports a holistic approach to helping individuals and families thrive. A financial and relationship coach, mentor, and board member. Tyra radiates joy as her life quest is "adulting with child-like wonder." https://www.facebook.com/synergyservicesnetworkllc

AFFIRMATION

I am filled with Joy. Joy is my source of strength, my God-given right, and my blessing to share.

Antonía Taylor

Antonía Lamoi Taylor is a Licensed Professional Counselor and a Soldier currently serving in the U.S. Army. She loves to write poetry and praise dance. If you ever meet her, you will never forget her.
Find her on FB @ https://www.facebook.com/annointedbaby or IG @ https://www.instagram.com/annointedbaby

AFFIRMATION

Bask in the warm embrace of love, allowing its radiant energy to illuminate your path to joy.

Felisha Taylor

Felisha Taylor was born and raised in rural Alabama. She is a proud mother to two young men. God reignited her childhood passion for writing after her divorce. She is a poet and author of a Divorce Devotional, titled *The Other Side*. She has plans to publish a series of children's books soon as well.

Email: othersidedivorce@gmail.com

AFFIRMATION

I am going to the other side.
Greet today with love!
My latter days are better than my former days.
God is here and around the corner.
God will autocorrect me; step out in faith.
I am becoming the best version of myself.
God can use everything for His glory.

Dr. Tschanna Taylor

Dr. Tschanna Taylor is a publishing and marketing consultant who teaches female entrepreneurs how to magnetize, monetize, and maximize their message using their books or chapters in book anthologies to produce money-making income streams. Connect with her on Facebook, Instagram, and TikTok. Visit her website at www.tschannataylor.com.

"I have told you this so that my joy may be in you and that your joy may be complete". John 15:11

AFFIRMATION

I decided to be joyful every day.

Evangelist Maria Terry

Evangelist Maria Terry is a two-time best-selling author, Evangelist Terry has studied under the leadership of Pastors Alfred and Susie Owens of Greater Mount Calvary Holy Church spreading the word and her love of Christ for 23 years through her charismatic and transparent approach.
FB: Maria Terry, Bounce Back group
Instagram: evangterry

AFFIRMATION

Psalm 32:8
I will structure thee and teach thee in thy way which thou shalt go: I will guide thee with mine eye. Bouncing back and doing it on purpose!

____

____

____

____

____

____

____

____

____

____

____

Joyan Thomas

I am Joyan Hutchinson I am from the parish of Manchester in Jamaica West Indies. I am the seventh of ten children. I attended St. Andrew Technical High School doing Commercial Studies. I worked in the USA as a Nursing Assistant. I am the mom of six beautiful children and six beautiful grandchildren. I love God. He is my everything.
Joyh20209@gmail.com

AFFIRMATION

Without God I am nothing. I will continue to praise and worship him. I know he is my provider, my giver, my love, and most of all, my Father. I know He will always be with me, in the darkest moment, because I was there, and He saved me and gave me a second chance in life. Amen

Choose Joy

Vera Thomas

Vera Thomas is a Life Coach, International Speaker, Trainer, Mediator, and Poet. 23x bestselling author and producer of a by-weekly podcast/radio show *The Vera Thomas Show*. She has worked with individuals, companies, non-profit organizations, schools, and churches engaging youth and adults.
Vera is available for companies who want to transform their teams or families who want to transform their lives.

AFFIRMATION

Today I let go and let the joy of the Lord be my strength. I am strong in the Lord and in the Power of His might. I am full of joy and peace. I react, relate, and respond in all situations with wisdom which brings me joy.

___

___

___

___

___

___

___

___

___

___

Darlene Thorne MDiv.

Pastor Darlene Thorne, MDiv, CEO of A Heart After the Father, LLC, guides women caregivers in holistic self-care. . Darlene and her husband Kevin pastor Renewal Community Church in Clayton, NC. Parents to two dynamic young adults, Kevin II, and Kennedy Elayne. Connect with Darlene Thorne via IG linktr.ee/Ladydarlene.

AFFIRMATION

My failures yesterday led me to my successes, I won't quit!
I will surround myself with positivity!
I will surround myself with motivated people!
My sphere of influence is growing!
I will spend time reading great books!
I am led by the spirit of God!
He alone is my strength!

Shawntia Thorpe

Shawntia Thorpe is a native of Greensboro, N. C, She is a mother to one son and caregiver to her Granma with a heart of gold, She is an Assistant Manager she can be found on fb@ShawntiaThorpe

AFFIRMATION

Within me is the power to create great experiences. I choose to take this power into my mind and focus on creating happy, fulfilling, and lasting positive experiences using God's word. So, I always stay joyful.

Shanee Tinnin

Shanee Tinnin is a resilient powerhouse and gunshot survivor. Shanee is a devoted mother of seven and a widow. Her unwavering strength led her to become a passionate humanitarian. Leveraging her psychology background, Shanee enlightens and empowers both youth and adults about the utmost importance of mental wellness.
For inquiries, contact her at Info@shaneetinnin.com.

AFFIRMATION

Foster a sense of wonder, opening your heart to the enchanting mysteries of life.

Nikkia Tisaby

"Coach Ky' Tisaby's most important mission is to erase the stigma regarding mental health She utilizes the lessons she has learned in her journey living with Bipolar Disorder. The Hu'Mend Network is a 501c3 non-profit ministry that provides life coaching to youth living with a mental disorder. In her book Beauty from Ashes: Finding Redemption in Self-forgiveness, she shares her testimony and details of how she survived suicide. The book also features a self-paced journal: 7 Principles to Self-Success from Distress

AFFIRMATION

"Forgiveness is the needle that mends the soul." God's love is unconditional and pure. When you choose to forgive, you are displaying that love to others. Choose the path less taken. Choose to love.

____

____

____

____

____

____

____

____

____

____

____

Viviana Torres

I go by Vivi and I have been a Floridian since I was 13 years old when we moved here from New York. I continue to learn and grow every day and I rejoice! Every day is a blessing.
For prayer requests, visit: linktr.ee/thebluelineangels

AFFIRMATION

Pray: Father God, thank You for the trials in my life. When invading thoughts or behaviors creep in, I pray for spiritual endurance. May I remember what Yeshua did for me at the cross. I am a daughter or son of the highest King. I give You all the glory, Amen.

Elyzon Tosin

Elyzon Tosin is a Clinical data analyst, Chemist, makeup artist, and the Convener of Shepillars- a non-profit she started for young girls, widows, DMV survivors, and women in under-served communities. Shepillars has held outreaches in New Jersey and recently in Africa. Check www.shepillars.org, IG- @shepillars @elyzonbay to learn more about the work she does.

AFFIRMATION

I am healing, grief doesn't define me for Christ in me is the hope of glory. Fear is defeated, I walk in authority and the fullness of his power. I bask in his goodness and mercies each day.
Every day is better and brighter because God is with me every step of the way.

Dr. Gloria Trueh

Dr. Gloria Trueh is the Founder and CEO of United Women Leaders Global Network, is a Business Coach and Consultant, International Speaker, Best-selling author, Entrepreneur, and Pastor. She is passionate, dedicated and with 20 years of leadership experience helps start-ups, and women transition from the corporate world to entrepreneurship.

AFFIRMATION

The Joy of the Lord is my strength.
My ability to conquer challenges is limitless.
I possess the qualities needed to be extremely successful.
My business is growing, and expanding, and I am thriving.
The Lord will surround me will favor like a shield.
My Help is in the Lord.

Suzette A. Tubi

Suzette A. Tubi is a highly dedicated childcare professional and preschool teacher with over thirty-five years of experience. She is also a Certified Nursing Assistant for pediatric and elderly patients. Her lifetime of ministerial experience began with her theological studies at Pneuma Bible Institute. She will soon graduate from Life Christian Bible Institute with a B.A.in Theology.
For 15 years, Suzette served as an ordained missionary at Mighty Move of God Deliverance Temple. Suzette lives with her husband, Mr. Jenrola Tubi in Stamford, CT. She is a mother of one son, who resides in California.

AFFIRMATION

I am a reflection of God's divine Joy.

Caren Tunget

Caren Tunget is an educator, health and wellness coach, wife, mother, and grandmother. Connect with her on Facebook or @salt.and.lite on Instagram.
Title: *Embraced by Grace: A Journey from Fear to Total Surrender*
So now the case is closed. There remains no accusing voice of condemnation against those who are joined in life union with Jesus, the Anointed One.

AFFIRMATION

I am joined in life-union with Jesus, empowered by His grace to live abundantly, and without accusation.

Dr. Rhonda Turner

Dr. Rhonda Williams-Turner an author, speaker, role model, mentor, and community leader for over 25 years. Mrs. Turner is the founder of 4 Knowledge is Power a nonprofit and holds a master's degree in Mental Health and Marriage & Family. She has faithfully worked to implement numerous youth and adult programs in her community.

www.4knowledgeispower.org
Facebook:
https://www.facebook.com/rhonda.williamsturner

AFFIRMATION

I have a reason for being because God has a purpose for my life. Today I live for my purpose but every day I live to please God.

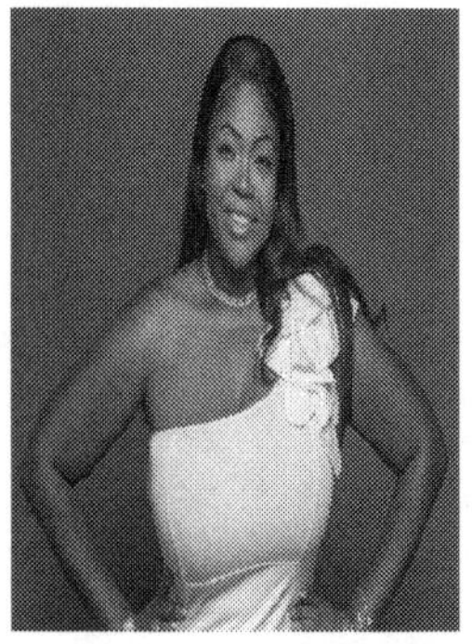

Tierra Turner

Tierra Turner is an exemplary figure of strength and determination as a Health and Wellness coach and motivational speaker. By the age of 33, she had already experienced the loss of both her parents. This profound grief became a catalyst for her journey towards finding strength in her faith.

AFFIRMATION

I embrace my journey to healing, finding strength in the face of trauma and grief. Through my pain, I discover resilience and growth on my path to healing. Grief may be heavy, but I carry it as a testament to my strength and capacity for healing.

Betty Tyler

Betty Tyler resides in Prince George County MD, Mother of 2, IT professional, Author, Community Advocate, Freelance writer, Encourager, Mentor, Civic leader, and Lay Christian Counselor-in-training
Facebook: bj.tyler.90
Instagram: bjctyler
LinkedIn: Betty Tyler
https://www.bettyjtyler.com

AFFIRMATION

Prayer:
Gracious father, I feel alone, but I know you are with me always. I know my emptiness is being filled by your loving spirit. Fill my hurting soul with your love and peace. Fill the emptiness and pain as only you can. Help me to walk in the fullness of your joy in Jesus' name. Amen

____

____

____

____

____

____

____

____

Tralyne Usry

Tralyne grew up in Augusta, Georgia, where she attended Paine College and earned her B.A. degree in Communications. She earned her Master's in Education from Ashford University in Clinton, Iowa. She is also a screenwriter and filmmaker, embarking on a project to produce her first feature-length film *Ebony & Ivory*!

AFFIRMATION

Your process is your pathway to the promise! You were made for this!
Nothing Can Stop You but You!
You are powerful! You were created by power! It's in your very makeup!
You ARE infinite potential and insurmountable possibilities!
YOU ARE (fill in the blank) NOW BE YOU!

Debra Valentine

Debra was born and raised in Tennessee. She graduated from Fisk University in Nashville, TN with a B.A. in Psychology and an M.A. in Educational Psychology/Counseling from Tennessee Technological University, Cookeville, TN. She served over 36 years within the TN state government. Mrs. Valentine is married to Dr. Donald R. Valentine, a Pastor in Oakland, KY. They were blessed with three children. Debra A. Valentine, Co-Author

dav.tine@live.com

AFFIRMATION

We all have life investments that lack adequate management. We should evaluate our gains and losses and release the clutter. God has plans for us to see, hear, and execute.

Carlica Villines

Carlica Villines is a dedicated mother with a diverse career journey, now thriving in an assembly plant. With a heart full of resilience, she's been a teacher, writer, and caregiver, channeling her multi-faceted skills into the precision of assembly work. Her dedication to family and work defines her remarkable story.

AFFIRMATION

"I am on a journey towards reuniting with my family, and I embrace each moment with gratitude. My heart finds joy in the present, and I trust in God's perfect timing. I am resilient, connected, and full of love, knowing that our reunion will be a beautiful blessing."

Chiquita Villines

Chiquita Villines is a professional caregiver and abundantly experienced trauma survivor, She is a creative writer with a wild imagination, open mind, and unique ability to make a major impact with her words, both verbally and in written format! After creating fiction novels just to unbottle and overcome transitioning from a teen parent to a parent of two teens, bouts of depression, poverty, and witnessing addiction; she has finally begun to share these works with the world. Chiquita has realized that her once "coping mechanism" is indeed actually her gift!

AFFIRMATION

I have allowed myself to move past the things and people who no longer bring positivity to my life. I can trust. I believe in Jesus; I can receive it. I realize peace is the most expensive thing on the menu.

Kenecia Villines

Kenecia Villines is a loving Mother, Caterer, and Chef who owns the Open Palette, She is a traveling chef and offers meal prep for special diets. She can be found on FB and IG @The Open Palette. She studied at Milwaukee Technical College.

AFFIRMATION

"I understand that true joy is a gift from my God. My joy reflects my spiritual connection and emotional well-being. I appreciate the diverse aspects that make up the anatomy of joy in my life and I consciously live therein".

Dr. Dorn J.B. Walker

Dr. Dorn J. B. Walker is a licensed ordained minister & seminary instructor. She partners with her husband Apostle John Walker, Jr., at "Walls of Salvation Church Ministries" in Pensacola, Florida. She authored "Life After Loss: A Journey into Wholeness", "School of True Worship and Effectual Fervent Prayer" & several ecclesiastical training products. www.wallsofsalvation.global

AFFIRMATION

God's thoughts toward me are of peace and not evil. I'm confident that I have a future and hope. I have a predestined purpose that I must fulfill. Therefore, I show up daily for my life. Every day, I immerse myself with God's Oil of Joy, His healing balm of liquid love that keeps me whole and restored!

Apostle John Walker., Th. D.

Apostle John Walker., Th. D. is the overseer of "Walls of Salvation Church Ministries" in Pensacola, Florida. He's on track to earn a Doctorate in Theology from The Empowerment Theological Institute & Bible Seminary in October 2023. His book *I Decree Your Apocalypse – Uncover Your* Mystery is scheduled for release in Fall 2023. www.wallsofsalvation.global

AFFIRMATION

Lord, you are my overflowing, Joy!
My Delight is in you, Lord!
Lord fill my joy, that my joy might be full, complete, wanting nothing!
I will not chase something that only the Lord God can fill.
Joy does not come from men but comes from the Lord.

Lisa Walton

Lisa D. Walton is a dedicated Army Veteran hailing from Washington D.C. With a strong commitment to her country, she has transitioned into a career in Budget and Finance, where she applies her discipline and expertise to ensure financial efficiency and success. Her service continues to make a difference.

AFFIRMATION

"I embrace life's storms, finding joy even in adversity. Like a dancer in the rain, I twirl through challenges with grace and joy. Adversity cannot extinguish the light of joy within me."

Lisa Washington

Lisa Washington, Known for her wit, candor, and passion, is a wanted Speaker, Interviewer, and Host. A DC native, Lisa has a connection to the local community that many rival. Whether volunteering with a young girl mentorship program or hosting a product launch party with DC's finest, Lisa's gift to gab and contagious energy sets the mood of the room. Visit www.lisadovewashington.com

AFFIRMATION

Today I will embrace all things good, bad, and indifferent and remind myself that my experiences serve as my testimony to how I can and will overcome! I will hold a stance of thankfulness each day and remember that all things happen to strengthen me and prepare me for my next!

Andrea Waters

Andrea Waters is an accomplished Career and Personal Development champion, with over 2 decades in the industry. Purposeful about her life's assignment. She is at her best when helping others tap into their unrecognized potential. Connect with her on FB (Andrea Waters) and at https://msha.ke/watersandco

AFFIRMATION

I affirm that my ability to work is a gift from God! I embrace my skills and talent as I contribute to the well-being of my family and my community. I am blessed to be a blessing and find joy in the work of my hands.

Dr. Melinda Watts

Dr. Melinda Watts is the Pastor of Integrity Int'l Worship Centers. She is known for her unique style of prophetic worship and preaching. She is married to Ronald Watts. They reside in Columbia Maryland. She is an author of the book *The Fire Couldn't Burn Me*. available on Amazon. cupofcoffeewithjesus88@gmail.com

AFFIRMATION

You got this!
Do not be dismayed, you just praise him anyway!
AGAIN, I SAY PRAISE HIM ANYWAY!

Cynthia Waugh

Cynthia Waugh is the tenth of eleven children. I was born and raised on the beautiful island of Jamaica, in the Caribbean. I am known as *'The Plant Whisperer'*. I studied Arts and General Studies in Secondary School. I love music, and I love to dance. *Horticulture* is my favorite hobby.

WhatsApp: Cynthia Vassell | Facebook: Cynthia Vassell

AFFIRMATION

I AM independent and self-sufficient. I AM not defined by my past. My body is healthy, strong, and beautiful. I AM not afraid of storms because I am learning how to sail my ship. Today I AM grateful to be alive and filled with serenity and happiness. I AM grateful for everything I have in my life.

Detra White-Cowan

Detra Cowan is a veteran and a business consultant/advisor providing price and cost analysis to small businesses. She is also a spiritual motivator and owns a gourmet popcorn business. Connect with her on Facebook, Detra White-Cowan, www.granmeres.com, or at www.prayinghandsministries.com.

AFFIRMATION

Embracing Change
It is through the process of change that sanctification begins.
It is through the process of change that I become spiritually mature.
It 'is through the process of change that I become spiritually equipped. It is through the process of change that God enlightens my heart.
It is through the process of change that strengthens my relationship with God.

Joann Weathersby

Joann Weathersby I'm a wife, mother, grandmother, great-grandmother, author, conference speaker, and most important of all. I am an ordained servant of God. My book *Proverbs 31: Woman a Peek into Her Past*, changed the trajectory of my life and walk with Jesus.

AFFIRMATION

You are who God says you are! Knowing your value and identity according to God's word, not the opinion of others is the difference between living a life of victory or walking in perpetual defeat. God declares your value to be "far above rubies." You are Proverbs 31.

Keith West

Keith West is a retired owner-operator who has transitioned into a life coach and author. Drawing from his experiences in the business world, he inspires me to guide others to achieve their goals and navigate life's challenges. Keith empowers individuals to reach their fullest potential. To contact Keith, you can email him via kewking53@gmail.com

AFFIRMATION

Embrace the transformative power of prayer, for it has guided my path and spoken life into existence. Trust in the ever-present nature of God, and let prayer be your source of strength. Together, we build a kingdom of faith and transformation. Remember, God is your constant guiding force.

____

____

____

____

____

____

____

____

____

____

____

Trish West

Trish West is a recognized mental health and addictions psychotherapist, a best-selling author, and an advocate for mental well-being. Her dynamic speaking engagements inspire and educate on a global scale, raising awareness for mental health and addiction issues.
For more information, visit her website: www.nistherapy.com.

AFFIRMATION

You are a beautiful soul, and your worth extends far beyond appearances or possessions. Embrace your inner qualities, self-confidence, and self-belief, for that is where true beauty resides. Remember, it's okay not to be okay; your journey is a testament to strength and self-acceptance. You radiate beauty from within.

C. Duane Wheeler

C. Duane Wheeler, the author of *To My Knowing* is now working on his second memoir. He believes his mission in life is to promote awareness through his writing. Whether it be Poetry or Novel, “I want my readers to see something enlightening, empowering, and sincere in the words I share. “You can find, *To My Knowing* on Amazon, called by readers “A true Southern classic, that reads like a song.”

AFFIRMATION

The Psalm Joy in Spirit was written about a note.
Of victory experienced after Duane was obedient in prayer.

Dr. Jenaya White

Dr, Jenaya White is a social entrepreneur, motivational speaker, international best-selling author, and award-winning community leader with a passion for helping girls and women become the best versions of themselves through her empowerment organization. Connect with her by visiting www.jenayawhite.com. You may also connect with her on all social media platforms with the social media handle: @drjenayawhite

AFFIRMATION

I am loved by God and He brings me joy.
My heart is open to receiving renewed joy and happiness.
I release all negative energy and welcome joy and positivity.
Joy flows through me freely and abundantly.
I trust in God's plan for my life, and I am filled with joy.

Stephanie White

Authoress SWD is energetic, straightforward, and family-oriented. Besides her authorship, she is an entrepreneur with several licenses, a poet, and a notary. linktr.ee/authoress_swd

AFFIRMATION

I am worthy, strong, and a conqueror. – Authoress SWD
My strength in faith always keeps me going – Authoress SWD
I choose greatness over mediocrity – Authoress SWD
Waking up is happiness to a fresh start – Authoress SWD
My daily living is perseverance – Authoress SWD

Tammi Whittman

Evangelist Whitman is an IT Specialist and a proud veteran who served the U.S. Army for 10 years. She is the wife of Rev. Antione Whittman, a mother, and grandmother who loves spending time with her family. Tammi's passion is ministry by way of mentoring and encouraging others. She currently works with women's prison ministry, encouraging women through bible studies, prayer, and encouragement.

AFFIRMATION

Every morning we wake up is a gift from God; everything we receive after that is a bonus so remember to give thanks!

Ivy Wilcox

Lady Ivy is a worshiper, mentor, intercessor, servant leader, and Minister of the faith.

Inspired by God, Lady Ivy founded the Women Designed with Purpose (WDWP) women's group in 2011. The mission of WDWP is to empower and encourage women to build healthy relationships while developing their God-given purpose.

AFFIRMATION

Difficult times will come, but I will not be defeated.
I will soar above my challenges and receive.
all that God has for me.
Wake up & trust God.
Walk around & see God's goodness.
Wait patiently; He will see you through.

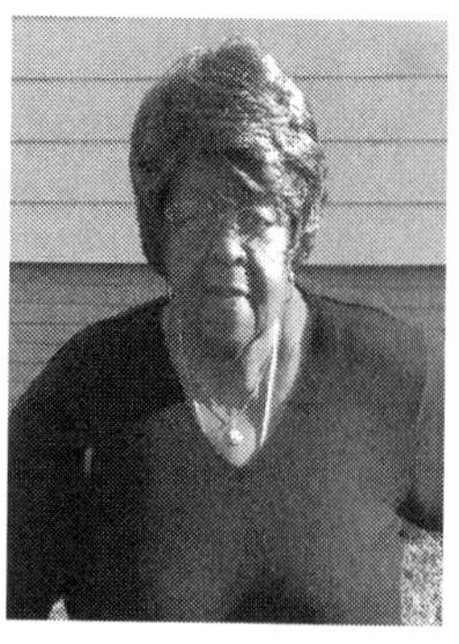

Annette Wiley

Annette Wiley was born in Person County NC and is a 83 yr old woman with a wealth of life experiences and wisdom. Retired from North Carolina Central University. She is the only living survivor out of 13 children, she is a Mom and Grandma and loving Auntie to many.

AFFIRMATION

In times of sorrow, I hold onto the divine promise of joy. I trust that joy will emerge even in the darkest moments of my life. God's promise of joy sustains me through all trials.

Belinda Wiley

Belinda Wiley I'm a dedicated wife, mother, grandmother (Ganna) sibling, friend, and prayer warrior, I'm also a proud daughter of the one true loving God, I sing with the Orange Grove Missionary Baptist Church Praise Team and Choir. I pray that my life serves as a testament to God's goodness and his faithfulness.

AFFIRMATION

I have joy like a river that never runs dry. My heart is constantly full of Joy, and it spreads through everything I do. Everything I touch becomes gold because I do what I do from a place of joy. I am joyful and I spread joy!

Maurice Wiley

Maurice Wiley I'm lovingly referred to as Tweety, Honey, Dad, Pops & PaPa. I spent 50 of my 60 years on earth trying to figure out who I am in my own way. It didn't work. Trying God showed me that I'm a son of the living God.

AFFIRMATION

I am fearfully and wonderfully made, with a unique purpose woven into the tapestry of my being by a loving Creator. In surrender to God, I find my identity and experience lasting joy.

Francine Williams

Francine Williams- I am an ordained Minister, Chaplain, and retired RN from the Dept of Education. I have devoted my life to providing practical solutions for troubled families, currently through lives on FB. I believe living life to the fullest is God's plan for us all.

AFFIRMATION

Daily application of the whole word Of God is crucial in meeting the needs of each human being, body, soul, and spirit. The foundation of the family is the basis of all institutions. God's plans for us have always been for good if we live for Him.

Tanya Butler Williams

Tanya Butler Williams is a first-time author, wife, mother, and grandmother who is deaf/and hard of hearing. Tanya is the creator of a family support group for parents and children who are deaf and hard of hearing. Using an unbiased approach, she teaches families to understand the uniqueness of their children.

AFFIRMATION

I am heard and understood when I communicate clearly and assertively. My voice and opinions hold value and importance, and God listens attentively.

Bobbie Willis

Bobbie Willis is a distinguished pastor and leader in the A.M.E. Zion church. I teach faith, healing, and how to have a spiritual relationship with God. I beat cancer and subdued other health challenges. I can be found online at www.facebook.com/revBobbieWillis.

AFFIRMATION

I have been crucified with Christ; it is no longer I who live, but Christ lives in me; and the life which I now live in the flesh I live by faith in the Son of God, who loved me and gave Himself for me. Galatians 2:20
Paul encourages us to let Christ live in us. He knew that we could be transformed by the renewing of our minds. Every time stress comes, and the challenges seem unbearable, speak as Paul spoke, “It’s not I who live, but Christ who is living in me.

Dawn Wilson

Dawn Wilson is married to her loving husband James of 22 years, Military Veteran of eight years, retired from the Department of Veterans Affairs, holds a degree in Business Management, Loves serving God, and doing all I can to bring Joy and light to those who cross my path.

AFFIRMATION

"So do not fear, for I am with you; do not be dismayed, for I am your God. I will strengthen you and help you; I will uphold you with my righteous right hand." Isaiah 41:10

James Wilson

James Wilson is a retired Army veteran. I currently work for the Department of Veterans Affairs, continuing my service for those who have served. I've been married to my loving wife, Dawn for 22 years and we currently have one dog.

AFFIRMATION

"I am purposeful for this life. Every day I rise, I will live the life I've been given."

Jae Joi Wingfield Ed.S., MCPC

Jae Joi is a life-long learner, educator, and Joiful Life Strategist and Leadership Coach. She finds her joy in cultivating meaningful relationships with her chosen community of diverse and eclectic humans. Jae calls the Atlanta area home and has lived there for several decades with her two (now adult) children. She is the author of *I Choose to be Joiful*, a self-love reflection journal available on Amazon.

AFFIRMATION

I will see the good in each day. I will embrace the lesson in each setback. I will remain hopeful for the future. I will be joyful.

Dr. Tonya T. Wise

Dr. Tonya T. Wise is an acclaimed international speaker, author, coach, and consultant, specializing in financial literacy, entrepreneurship, and money management.

Contact her at
https://www.tonyatwise.com | https://www.tonyatwise.com
Email: tonya@tonyatwise.com
Facebook: Allnewbeginngs
LinkedIn: tonyatwisecoach
Instagram: tonyatwise

AFFIRMATION

I embrace the harmony of faith and profession. Trusting in the Lord's guidance, I release control, surrender to divine wisdom, and align my multifaceted nature with His purpose. Empowered by His strength, guided by His wisdom, I bring glory to His name, making a positive impact in the world. Amen.

Dasia Wood

Dasia Wood is passionate about mental well-being and providing mental health resources. I also spread the gospel and incorporate the word in my mental health outreach. I aspire to be a mental health professional who encourages and uplifts many people through my purpose and work.

AFFIRMATION

If we are only joyful during the few major moments and events in life, then we will only be able to feel joyful sometimes. If we find and choose joy in all areas of life, we can be joyful a countless number of times. Joy can't depend on circumstances, or it will be limited. Joy comes from God, and we can choose to recognize joy and positivity in all areas of life rain or shine. That way our joy can be limitless.

Melissa Wood

Melissa Wood is an accountant who has recently been called to write what God has done in her and through her, as well as share how He has brought her through. You can connect with her on Facebook (https://www.facebook.com/missyk334/)

AFFIRMATION

Trials come in many shapes and sizes during our lives. However, when we live with our spiritual roots deeply grounded, we may bend in the presence of the storm, but we will never break.

Dr. Rhonda Wood

Dr. Rhonda Wood is an award-winning international speaker, bestselling author, purpose coach, and leading authority on mental health. She champions women, empowering them to "heal out loud" and rediscover their worth, purpose, and passion. Rhonda boldly speaks out in a culture where women are expected to remain silent.
Connect with her at https://DrRhondaMWood.com or @DrRhondaMWood.

AFFIRMATION

I am a vessel of God's joy, and my life reflects His love and goodness. As I journey through life's seasons, I carry the banner of joy, reminding myself and others that true happiness springs from within and reflects my faith in God. Today and every day, I choose to honor, embrace, and share God's joy.

Matrice Woodall

Matrice C. Woodall is a published author. She loves writing meaningful poems and enjoys spoken word events. Music is a rhythm to many things, she believes. Deep conversation and inspirational writing stimulate the soul. She loves deeply and wants the best for others.

AFFIRMATION

I am strong and independent.
I am above and not beneath.
I am favored by God.
I am making great strides to be the best version of me.
I am putting my health and mental health first.
I am beautiful just the way I am.

____

____

____

____

____

____

____

____

____

____

____

April Woolsey

April Woolsey I'm from Columbia, SC. I proudly served my country in the US Army as an engineer for nine years with a tour in Iraq. I became a widow at 24, and I am a member of the Gold Star Wives. I have two degrees in the Criminal Justice field, and I love the outdoors.
FB: https://www.facebook.com/april.jones.984
IG: aj.sappermama

AFFIRMATION

Always tell yourself that no matter how hard life gets, you will make it!! Stay strong and believe in yourself and what you're capable of. Focus on your well-being, and most of all, live for you! Self-care is the best medicine for the soul!

Dr. Iris Wright

Dr. Iris Wright is a wife, mother, entrepreneur, published author, and speaker. Connect with her on Facebook, Author Iris Wright, and iris-wright.com.

AFFIRMATION

I am surrounded by God's infinite love and protection every moment of my life. I trust in the divine power to guide me towards my highest good and to keep me safe from all harm. I release all fear and doubt and fully surrender to the grace of God. I am grateful for the blessings that come my way and I know that every challenge is an opportunity for growth and learning. I am confident in my ability to overcome any obstacle with God's love and support. I affirm that I am always on the right path and that I am fulfilling my divine purpose. Thank you, God, for your unwavering love and protection.

Joyce Wright

Joyce Wrigt was born and raised in East Orange, New Jersey. Joyce's love for Christ started at a young age. when She attended Beulah Baptist Church in Newark New Jersey. Joyce is a grieving Mother who lost two children Sakeenah and Omar. When not writing, Joyce enjoys shopping, traveling, and attending church gatherings. Connect with Joyce on FB @ or email joycewright1234@gmail.com

AFFIRMATION

I dwell in the presence of my Father. Therefore, I enjoy comfort, peace of mind, direction, and speed in my healing process.

Shadawn Wright

Shadawn Wright (MSW, MPA) is a native of Hollywood, SC. She works in the field of Social Work. Shadawn is the author of a *3 Day Devotion titled, "Don't Look Back, Let It Go!"*. She currently lives in Augusta, Georgia. Shadawn enjoys spending time with family, reading, and traveling.

AFFIRMATION

I challenge you this day to STOP allowing fear to hold you back from completing God's assignment. If God gave you the vision, he has equipped you to carry it out. Why are you still sitting there? Go ahead and fulfill your purpose. God's waiting!

Dr. Angela White-Stephens

Dr. Angela White-Stephens is an ordained Elder still grounded and standing on her southern roots to serve in the church. A dedicated Christian serving others and teaching the Word of God. She models the behavior that she teaches others to demonstrate. Dr. White-Stephens is very passionate about understanding and serving God.

AFFIRMATION

Prayer: Dear Heavenly Father, thank you for your unconditional love, your goodness, and your loving kindness to me and all that are called by your name. And I Praise you and you alone are worthy. Great is your faithfulness and I praise you for you alone are worthy. Help me to wait patiently for you in humble submission to your Holy Spirit in Jesus name Amen.

Danyell Winkey-Smith

Danyell Winkey Smith is a Maryland resident, A wife, mother, and grandmother. A Community Advocate/Organizer, a retired Federal Employee. Served on the Baltimore County Democratic State Central Committee.

AFFIRMATION

For once you forgive, you are free to live a life full of Peace and JOY. I found my Joy in Gratitude because God saved me. I found my Joy in Living because I almost lost it. I found my Joy in Family and Friends because they love unconditionally. I found my Joy in Loving Again because I thought my heart was broken. I found my Joy in Giving because I love seeing people smile. I found my Joy in Sharing my Story because it sometimes saves lives. I found my Joy in Laughing Again because it used to hurt. I found my Joy in Kindness because it truly matters. I found my Joy because God loved me and forgave me. John 15:11 "These things I have spoken to you, that my joy may be in you, and that your joy may be full.

Debra Woodley Thomas

Debra Woodley Thomas, a native of Trinidad and Tobago, lives in Tennessee with her retired Army veteran spouse. A faith-filled, creative, and entrepreneurial military spouse, mother, and grandmother, she is a world traveler. Her roles as a partner, entrepreneur, and creative collaborator have made her who she is today. Https://www.facebook.com/debra.w.thomas.1?mibextid=nwBsNb

AFFIRMATION

Today, I will stand still and trust God. Today, I acknowledge He is in control and will care for me. I put my faith in Him and trust Him to do amazing things. "God, I surrender all to you!"

Blessings Joy 365 Community!!

We have shared affirmations with you from 365 Phenomenal Coauthors from all around the world. We pray these Affirmations Bless you and restore your joy. If this guide blesses you, please share it with others and be so kind to leave us a review. Coordinating this project has been none other than amazing.

To my coauthors keep soaring the sky is the limit, if this is your first book or fifth book or anywhere in between Congratulations on becoming #1 Best Selling Author with 364 others {please keep writing.} Keep being amazing on purpose and know that you will always have a special place in my heart.

Thanks for joining me in Joy 365!!!
Love you.
Dr. Vee